TOGETHER WE CAN DO SOMETHING WONDERFUL

How To Harness The Power Of Collaboration

GILL TINEY

WM

Together We Can Do Something Wonderful

First published in September 2021

W&M Publishing

ISBN 978-1-912774-99-9 ebk

ISBN 978-1-912774-98-2 pbk

A CIP catalogue record for this book is available from the British Library.

Where necessary, all people mentioned in case studies have been used with permission, and/or have had names, genders, industries and personal details altered to ensure client confidentiality.

Contents

Here's Why

"None of us, including me, ever do great things.
But we can all do small things, with great love,
and together we can do something wonderful."

Mother Teresa

What People Are Saying About This Book

At a time when collaboration is needed more than ever, here is a book that simply and clearly outlines the easiest way to achieve the best of outcomes.

According to Gill Tiney a true collaboration brings benefits not only to those who participate but also to the wider community as the 'pay it forward' culture takes hold.

Simon Anholt

Founder of The Good Country Index and the Global Vote; Independent Policy Advisor to Heads of State and CEOs; Speaker; Author & Researcher; Hon. Professor UEA.

We all need a little bit of Gill in our lives. I feel like Gill and I were always meant to meet and that first meeting ended up being for, no coincidence, a collaborative project. I've always deeply believed we can achieve more in life and in business through collaboration but never really truly known how to maximise that. Gill very clearly maps out that missing piece of the jigsaw so we can all work towards a better place to be.

Phil Street

Phil is a recruitment specialist and he is known for being honest, engaging, quality focused and relentless Focused on the hospitality sector he founded Momentum to get people moving. Also host of podcast Hospitality Meets....

The title of this book, and a quote from Mother Teresa says it all. Indeed, we can achieve extraordinary things to make a difference in the world, for the world, as a collective of light-minded individuals with a shared mission and purpose. Imagine the waves we can create if every single one of us throws a pebble in a pond at exactly the same time. I believe, now, no more than at any other time, we have a duty to create transformational as a collective, a tribe where we feel we belong and can be the best version of ourselves where we gain peace by accepting ourselves and others. Let's create a legacy for those who have sacrificed as we emerge from the impact of a global pandemic that has impacted upon our world like no other. This book shows you how!

Dr Lizzy Bernthal

Founder of Release Your Potential Ltd She has led and mentored multi-national and multi-functional teams in UK and abroad in Europe, Hong Kong and Saudi Arabia in a variety of contexts, organisations and cultures.

If you want to discover the power of collaboration and connection in your business and your life. If you are looking to create and sustain high levels of success and fulfilment, *Together We Can Do Something Wonderful* is a must-read and a complete game-changer.

Gina Gardiner

Two-Time #1 International Best Selling author, Motivational speaker, Empowerment Coach, Transformational Leadership Trainer, NLP Master

As soon as I met Gill and some of the fellow collaborators, I immediately got the feeling that things were about to get extremely interesting. Move just over one year and the world has morphed in such a way that it is starting to feel the impact of exactly what *Collaboration Global* is all about: association, participation, partnership and teamwork. Gill Tiney, in my view, is a catalyst who inspires and has joined the ranks of the trailblazers who form the paths along which we meander and tread throughout our lives. *Collaboration Global* will be a testament to what we leave behind.

Maria Azcona

Health and Safety Consultant at Risk Reports, Enterprise Advisor for Khalsa Academy, Stoke Pogues & Trustee for Collett School (SEND), part of The Blue Tangerine Consortium

For those who truly collaborate, it is an effortless fluid process. Connections form, rapport is built and relationships flow and develop. We are however all human, and sometimes even the best of us need a nudge in the right direction, or a reminder how to best channel our energies to get the very best experience out of life. Gill Tiney's current book "Together We Can Do Something Wonderful" is a deep dive into the technicalities of collaboration. It breaks down in simplistic terms, what we all to often take for granted, and delivers the contents in an easy to read, accessible and usable format. 100% well worth a read for anyone who is looking to grow in an authentic and truly present manner, to meet the challenge of being the very best version of themselves that they can be.

David Liddle

Ultra runner, cyclist mortgage and protection adviser. A Collaboration Catalyst and proud Scout Master.

I've observed how Gill Tiney is passionate about two main life themes: her biological family, and collaboration. In the true sense of a visionary, Gill sees a future where people are self-aware, who choose to work together for the betterment of all. That is one amazing mission, the theme of this book. Read it!

Benn Abdy-Collins

THE LISTENING GUY ... the One to Talk to, when you Really Need to Be Heard. Life Transitions Guide, Civil Funeral Celebrant, Medical Herbalist, Professional Speaker and Wordsmith.

Collaboration is natural, intuitive and the sustainable approach to life. We see it throughout the cosmos and in every facet and system upon our precious earth. Gill Tiney is a living example, reminding us of this powerful wisdom being the vital aspect and foundation of our personal and collective wellbeing. She guides us through her insights, experience and practical application to show how collaboration leads to thriving in every possible way. Beginning within, through self-awareness, she establishes how to tap this amazing innate potential and expands our perspectives to see how this encourages fresh ideas, opportunities and solutions that benefit all.

Harold W. Becker

Author and Founder, The Love Foundation

Foreword

James Knight

Entrepreneur, behavioural scientist, international speaker and creator of iMA a universal language of connectivity that allows communication to be harmonised across the world.

I have spent over 30 years researching, testing, applying and teaching a universal colour-based language I created called iMA that is designed to help people connect.

Sometimes when doing a group presentation introducing iMA I ask this question, *Has this ever happened to you when you met someone for only a couple of minutes and yet you felt so comfortable with that person that it seems like you have known them for years?*

That happened to me on August 14 2008, when I had the good fortune to be introduced to Gill Tiney by Penny Power OBE at an Ecademy Event, in London.

Gill is a dynamic, self actualizing individual with endless drive and energy and a genuine concern about the well-being of others.

We connected and have been working together in various ways for our mutual benefit ever since.

When it comes to the art and science of collaboration there isn't anyone that I know more qualified to teach you the principles, fundamentals and concepts that when practiced can help change your life for the better.

Over the past 25 years Gill has travelled the world networking and speaking at conferences, inspiring individuals, groups and organizations to become better at what they are doing by *Reaching in, Reaching out and Reaching together.* Helping to create an environment where people feel valued.

I encourage you to learn more about Gill Tiney and after you read this book, to learn more about the *Collaboration Global* Community that she founded and of which I am a member.

Here you will find a community covered under an umbrella of positive acceptance and approval.

The emphasis is placed on sincere appreciation for the good that people are doing.

Helping members help each other and themselves to *Be, Do and Live* better.

James Knight

What Is Collaboration?

The definition of *collaboration* according to *Collaboration Global*:

When three or more people come together
to create something of significance
that will positively impact the collaborators
and those who connect with them,
bringing a space of harmony and love.

Preface

As you can imagine *collaboration* is a behemoth to understand, decipher and articulate.

This is not my first attempt at extolling the virtues of collaboration. I have previously written *Making Of A Movement,* part of my initial foray into the collaborative world, when I co-founded *BeCollaboration.* That book focused on the context of collaboration and the levels at which it could have an impact.

Many of the areas I touch upon in this book are explored more fully in the *Making Of A Movement* book, to give you a better understanding of why I find it so powerful to harness the incredible tool of collaboration we all have at our fingertips.

You do not need to have read the previous book to get value out of this one.

The previous book talks about *why* we should collaborate, and, importantly, this book tells you *how.*

Obviously, I will also explain why collaboration is so valuable in this book too - I simply can't help myself. However, the main purpose of writing this book was so that everyone could access a really simple way of collaborating, so they could create a bigger impact.

Everyone *can* do it - and in my opinion, everyone *should* do it, and when you can create that success again and again you won't want to operate in any other way.

It is the gateway to saving our planet, but first we have to save ourselves.

Introduction

Collaboration is the new buzz-word. We hear it in most industries - collaborations are anticipated and occasionally come to fruition, but few appear to collaborate as a matter of course - except perhaps in the music industry. In my experience of the SME (Small Medium Enterprise) world, it is unlikely to be the case and many people, having been unsuccessful in a collaboration, are loath to try again.

Why is this?

On the face of it, a collaboration in business should create the perfect win/win for everyone involved, yet we often find it so hard to deliver an outcome we both want.

In my previous book, *Making Of A Movement*, I illustrate that historically, we, as a society, have been taught to look after number one. Our education system, political system, mainstream media, even the monetary system all pull for separation, however we have an innate desire that instinctively wants to collaborate.

Yet we appear to have forgotten how, our attempts to collaborate have become fraught with tension. In a society where we have been mainly taught to look out for number one, where it feels like a dog eat dog world and as Darwin pontificated that it is the survival of the fittest, we become wary of letting down our guard to collaborate.

I believe that now, like no other time in history, is the time to redress the balance. We are now open to what can be achieved when we come together, because of what we have been through together, globally through Covid19.

During the past decade I have been studying, researching and experimenting with the concept of utilising collaboration for a bigger purpose. Sure, you can use it to make more money, but that isn't what the world needs right now - bear with me for a moment, I can hear you saying you could actually do with some more cash. In the Western World, in circulation we actually have enough money, it simply isn't evenly distributed. What we need is harmony and from my learning I know that true collaboration can bring us that harmony; for an individual like you and me, to a group like your family, to a wider community and ultimately to a global society.

This book is a piece of the puzzle to illustrate how simple it can be to transform a culture to make collaborations simple and free flowing. I want to explain the benefits of collaboration, the fundamentals of a collaborative mindset and an understanding of the behaviours of a collaborative team. Once you have this understanding it will have a huge and lasting impact in practically every area of your life. I've experienced it myself and seen a transformation in others.

Collaboration is the answer to everything!

Yes, a bold statement, but let's just think of that for a minute...

What if politicians had been solution focused over the Brexit issue? Not looking to undermine, gain advantage, manipulate the situation for personal gain - on both sides.

What if there weren't actually sides? Many political systems around the world that believe in democracy are predicated on Right or Wrong - Left or Right as though one party has all the answers, when they clearly don't. How refreshing would it be for a politician to acknowledge they didn't have the answer and would go and find out, instead of playing the avoiding game and never actually answering a question. If the media didn't hound them for not knowing perhaps they wouldn't see a need to use so many words saying absolutely nothing, causing much frustration, it is such a vicious circle!

Ultimately, this results in a lose/lose situation for all concerned.

Imagine if they were working with a collaborative mindset and were solution focused, what might they have achieved? If they had been working collaboratively within the framework suggested in this book, I believe we could achieve many difficult transitions and create a positive outcome much sooner. This is how powerful I know the collaborative mindset is - imagine what it can do for your business!

Suffice to say, if more people were able to truly collaborate then more solutions would be sought, and the world could transform into a better place.

I believe it really is that simple.

However, at the moment, in my experience of running a collaborative organisation and, despite it being an innate human need, we, in the Western world are pretty bad at collaborating successfully.

This book aims to rectify that by sharing, in the simplest form, what is required in a good collaborative team and how, with that understanding, you can see a positive impact in every area of your life. The more people who understand the power and implementation of a collaborative mindset, the quicker we can help those currently suffering in our world.

This is just the beginning!

If *Saving The World* isn't on your agenda right now, then know that by understanding collaboration you will develop closer relationships, have less stress in your life, discover more free time, feel more content with life and ultimately be more successful - however that looks for you.

Make true collaboration part of your psyche even if you only apply it to a small part of your life and you will see that area transform!

This book is split into three parts.

- **Step 1** looks at your personal development and how you can create a great mindset for this collaboration.
- **Step 2** looks at the implementation into your business or place of work. And,
- **Step 3** illustrates how you can take your learning out to the wider arena and be part of the growing movement to support others through collaboration.

Truly being part of the change you want to see in our world.

Step One

Develop A Better Understanding of YOU!

Self-awareness, an essential
for great collaborations!

How to be your best YOU!

Chapter 1

IT STARTS - WITH YOU!

One day as I jumped out of my car to go to a meeting, I saw my friend getting out of her car, I waved and called over, "Hi Fi, how are you?"

She replied sarcastically, "I'm perfectly fine, *it's all them others that are the problem!"*

She laughed, but to her it was true. Other people caused all her problems, she was totally innocent and 'they' were hellbent on spoiling her happiness.

Ever felt like that?

If only everyone did what they were supposed to do, then I would be OK. If only my husband did the washing up, if only my kids tidied up after themselves, if only my boss was a better human being, if only my business partner listened to what I was saying... And then everything would be OK. I could be more productive, I could have less stress, I could enjoy my life more, I could be happy.

If it wasn't for all of them! (Notice the common denominator?)

It is way too easy to look at another human being and blame them for your situation, as if they are powerful enough to be responsible for your happiness. It is much harder to look inwards and see how you are sabotaging your own success and happiness. It is work we all need to do so that we can be awake to what controls us, to understand how we generate our thoughts and how debilitating our belief system can be when not founded on empowerment for ourselves and others.

For collaboration to truly work you must have a certain level of self-awareness, an understanding of what makes you tick, your motivations, your weak spots, your upsets and your blind spots, therefore every collaboration - in ANY area of your life, starts with YOU!

Don't misunderstand, we ALL have work to do because we have all been influenced in our lives by our circumstances, the nurture over nature debate. We have been taught what to believe by our parents and those around us, our natural instinct is to connect with others, as social animals we want to be part of a tribe, we have a need to fit in and so we build our belief system - whether it serves us or not.

It takes courage to begin the journey of self-discovery, to peel the layers of our complicated lives away until we are stripped bare of other people's input into our lives and see ourselves for who we truly are. For some it is a glorious path to freedom, for others it is a difficult road to redemption. Both journeys are well worth the effort, for the rewards are endless. The journey is an ongoing one - we are never done. Self-awareness is a holy grail to successful collaboration.

Let me briefly explain how you have possibly come to have your current outlook on life.

Where you were born had some indication of how well you might flourish. How financially comfortable your parents were suggested certain viewpoints might have been held. If you were not exposed to a different way of life your opinions/ beliefs may never have been challenged. Like learning a new language, it is difficult to be fluent unless you live in that community. Likewise, if you only ever experience a private education and followed father into the law via Oxbridge then it was unlikely you would have experienced the hand to mouth existence of some local authority housing tenants. Both experiences were valid and valuable in the university of life but not always under your control.

So, despite being born in the same country, very different belief systems would have been laid down. Even within the school you attended, there would have been further segregation and potentially more limiting beliefs being unconsciously embedded.

Throughout your education you were probably segregated - top set in Maths, bottom set in Literacy? Academics this way, athletes that way. In my primary school we were even segregated at playtime - boys in one playground, girls in another. Every year you were assessed and graded, always striving for that next piece of paper to get you on the next rung of this never-ending ladder. Get to work and more of the same, segregated by income, offices, title, and position. Remember your place!

Add in our media, promoting how to look, dress, what to watch and listen to. When I was 15, if you voluntarily wanted to listen to classical music you were deemed weird and scorned. We are all seeking to belong, to be accepted in some form and we do whatever we can to fit in.

Continue the view of separation, consider how money is viewed in our society. For many, mortgages are required, home ownership essential and you begin to realise we are shoe-horned into seeing our happiness as a direct correlation to our financial success. These examples are just a tip of the iceberg, we are conditioned into our consumerist societies.

What has that society created for us today?

Certainly, technology has given us more opportunities to be connected, and yet never has there been a higher rate of depression caused, in my opinion, by loneliness and a lack of true authentic connection.

We have more money in circulation than at any other time in our history and yet we have food banks in practically every town in the UK - my parents if they were still alive would be horrified.

We were promised more leisure time, but we now work 24/7 as our business follows us on our smartphone - not so smart, eh?

Life is changing so fast we don't know what is 'the best' anymore, what we *should* be using for optimum results, how we can be a 'success'.

Life used to be so sure, how to sell, where to market, who to employ, how to date, whom to love. Now it feels that the wider world is scary and confusing - fake news, conspiracy theories, terrorist attacks, pandemics, shall we just stay at home and be safe? Ironically, a choice imposed upon us.

We are constantly being fed a paradigm of fear, scarcity, and competition. Live in that space and it's easy to end up isolated and lonely, potentially leading to anxiety and depression.

How do you take the uncertainty of our current world and create something that will positively impact you, your corner of the planet and our society in general?

We can transform that old paradigm and create a new one of love, connection, and abundance.

Imagine what that world would look like!

Collaboration Is Key

What has been your experience of collaboration so far?

- Maybe a business arrangement didn't go so well.
- Possibly you worked within an established group and the ground rules weren't set.
- You found people were unreliable, never doing what they said they would.
- Do you believe there is always a hidden agenda?
- Office politics plays its part.
- People aren't prepared to be generous of their time or experience if they feel it jeopardises their position within the company.
- Or maybe, you feel the hassle and upset often caused, isn't worth the effort.

So, you have sworn off collaborating. It's much easier to go it alone. Or is it?

That used to be me, I'd get let down and I can hear myself saying, *Oh for goodness' sake, I might as well do it myself, it will be quicker,* but that attitude didn't serve me, in fact I was in danger of ostracising the people around me and isolating myself, because I took on a greater and greater workload and practically martyred myself, but at the time I just didn't see it.

Let's take a look at the logic of DIY; what are the challenges and benefits of going it alone?

- You have to be jack of all trades'.
- You *definitely* work harder.
- Your ideas have no one to bounce off to create new ideas.
- It can be lonely.
- Not so much fun - no banter.
- Can only support a smaller network.
- Maybe not earn as much.
- Can't share - ideas/products/clients/data/technology.
- Can't easily create lasting relationships with people who are aligned.
- You could end up distrusting everyone.
- But you get the job done, right? ...sometimes.
- No one to see you not achieve - not the best incentive.

How is that working out for you?

Let's acknowledge that going it alone can be tough and

that collaborating with others who are like you - generous, supportive, reliable, fun, engaging, creative and hardworking, would be an exciting scenario.

What would that collaboration look like?

Now, let's imagine that for a minute:

- Going to work every day would be a joy.
- Being able to rely on people without chasing them would be zero stress.
- Creating new ideas in your areas of genius.
- Putting them into action together would be energising.
- Having someone around who has your back would be reassuring.
- Not having to chase or chastise anyone because you could see they are all proud of their work and are putting all of their best work into it.
- Being proud of the outcome.
- Being grateful of the new relationships you have discovered.
- Being aligned with a cracking team of people working in their genius.
- Seeing potential from every area of the team.
- Feeling confident of every member and knowing they will ask for help if they are struggling.
- Enjoying clever banter.
- Socialising with your fab team.
- Work wouldn't feel like work.

- Earning your true value.
- Being seen by your peers as successful and your boss too.
- Being happy.
- Spreading happiness.
- Going to work every day would be a joy - worth saying twice.

So, can you see how collaboration, when it works, is amazing? Now all you need to do is understand the magic ingredients to creating the type of collaboration I've described and you are set for a whole new way of life - it is THAT powerful.

Plus, when we create powerful collaborations in our life and business don't you think we can pay it forward and help others in their life too? It becomes a triple win - for you, your business/career and for the planet. More on that later.

Now, to examine our self-awareness we can ask ourselves some useful questions.

- Do I have any triggers?
- What are my limiting beliefs?
- Do I understand what my genius is?
- What will I bring to a collaboration?

Earlier, we looked at some of the past experiences, or external factors contributing to our current belief systems, so, what we need to do is provide ourselves with a relatively clean slate, an open heart and headspace if you will, for working with others so that collaborations have a better chance of working.

Consider what that clean slate looks like.

Imagine if you were unaware of *Right* or *Wrong*. Being opinion free is also an empowering exercise. If we are not entrenched in opinion and are not committed to being right, we can open up a whole new world of possibility.

You may have heard the expression 'leave your ego at the door', but identifying our ego in every conversation requires a great deal of maturity and an ability to step away from our need to always be right. This takes practice and is easier for some than for others. What is pulling you to be right, why do you need the validation of being right, or proving someone else wrong? This stubborn attachment to habits or prejudices will not work in a collaborative environment.

Don't get me wrong (ha ha, did ya see what I did there?) You are still allowed to have an opinion, but a deep-rooted belief that you are always right is not empowering to everyone else. Have your thoughts, but don't be tied to them and engage with what else might be possible. It is a change of energy; a solution-focused space rather than a binary system of stop or go, right or wrong, black or white. Being pedantic in a collaborative endeavour will damage the project.

Even if you are *right*, throwing your weight around and bringing negative or aggressive energy into the room will not support the team going forward.

I once undertook a collaboration with six other business coaches. Pooling our diverse talents and creating a product to enhance each other's portfolio of products seemed a great idea. Sadly, it was an exercise in herding cats. At each meeting they took it in turns to illustrate their knowledge to the room, not necessarily enhancing the presentation of the previous person. Each meeting felt like a stand-alone, mini show-off session.

Certainly there was much value in the room but because of the illusion of superiority and on occasion not feeling it necessary to deign to show up and contribute in a practical way it quickly disintegrated.

Such a waste and such a shame. Part of my learning curve for sure.

This wasn't just about the egos in the room - of which there were plenty. It was also about assumptions made, no ground rules being established, no time line and no outcomes being laid out - apart from the potential income and how it would be distributed. Sadly, 40% of £0 is still £0.

If they had come to the sessions with a focused attitude of what can I do to help rather than the list of what they were not prepared to do, we might have created an amazing collaboration.

However, I am grateful for the experience as I learned so much about what NOT to do, because their ego walked into the room first.

Having an understanding of that ego voice inside our heads, where it comes from, what it sounds like, and how you can dissipate the noise stands us in good stead.

Collaboration In Action

An exercise to practice your self-awareness around your ego would be to spot the times when you speak from a place of making someone wrong purely to make yourself look good.

When you are in a meeting, or even talking with your children, can you spot whether your contribution is uplifting to the other person? Have you spoken from your ego? Or does what you say add depth, awareness and support a solution to the situation?

Try it for a day.

Every time you are in conversation, are you purposefully empowering another human to greatness?

Acknowledge people for their contributions.

Supportively challenge their conceptions without making yourself right.

Bite your tongue before you speak to prove yourself right - will it enhance the conversation? (Consider whether you are just doing it to make yourself feel good?)

At work or at play, if you have a habit of making people wrong - especially your family, can you pull back from that and empower them instead?

It may not happen overnight, but if you practice spotting when your ego is doing the thinking and speaking, instead of your truest self, you can transform that instinct. After a week or two, you can begin to look at those around you and you will start to witness them blossom. It is a beautiful thing. But this is still only part of the collaborative journey.

Chapter 2

COLLABORATION IS KEY TO YOU BECOMING YOUR BEST SELF

We were attending a business launch at a very swish London address, with glasses of bubbly and inspiring speeches. A new business had been born in our community when a member had an epiphany. He had bought a domain name ten years earlier and done nothing with it, until he saw the light at one of our *Collaboration Global* meetings and announced he was going to create a fabulous business. Fast forward six months and here we were celebrating with him.

The room was filled with our members, along with people in his industry and his investors. It was a high-octane environment, not the usual open and authentic space we had become used to. Everyone I spoke to was interested in my connection to the host, how was business, what did I do and, ultimately, how I might be useful to them. It was pretty exhausting not having a meaningful and interesting conversation, just lots of superficial enquiry.

When one of our members was verbally pinned in a corner and quite aggressively (alcohol was flowing) asked why she was part of our community, I was intrigued not only by what she would say, but by how she would respond to such a dismissive and rude attitude. I could not have been prouder. This gentle, kind, beautiful woman took a moment to consider, gazed to the ceiling in thought, made the man wait patiently for her reply and, with a beaming, disarming smile, replied, 'Simply to be the best me that I can possibly be.'

He was lost for words, his body language transformed dramatically, his aggressive stance disappeared and he became genuinely interested in the following conversation. He had heard something that was alien to him; collaborations in the past had cost him money, he didn't get how it would work or why. In that one sentence he saw possibility. She hadn't tried to justify herself, put a price on what she was getting out of it, or gushed about the lovely people in the group, she had been authentic, vulnerable and open, which in turn had created a profound impact on this man. The culture we had created of love, connection and abundance was now transcending our meetings and becoming visible to others outside of our community. Her quote, in its simplicity, sums up exactly what we had created.

How can you even start to contemplate a collaboration if you are so full of your own self-importance that you dismiss the possibility that you can grow and learn from others? I think we can probably all think of someone who believes they are superior - to you or others. If you are in a collaborative team and that person is sitting opposite and they take a superior stance, do you feel you will be able to give of your best?

Of course not.

My mind turns to politics. Imagine being in a room with Donald Trump and you want to give an opinion that you know he will not be open to - well, I guess we can all imagine how that might go.

I have experienced many people who needed to make me feel inferior to them. I remember one car journey where I was in the back with two colleagues in the front, one posed a question and I gave my opinion, which both immediately dismissed as 'ridiculous'. The conversation continued for a full 20 minutes while they talked through options and eventually one came to his definitive solution, which was exactly what I had said in the very beginning. I cannot deny that I took great pleasure (my ego) in reminding them of the fact.

What if their egos, their need to be better than me, had been put to one side while they at least considered what I had said? At the very least, by being open, self-aware and not self-important, they could have saved 20 minutes. Worse, if they had not had that time in the car to contain the conversation, they might never have achieved a solution.

Learn from others - be open to what you hear. It may not resonate with you immediately, but by considering what might be possible it gives new questions which move you towards new solutions. Looking for new solutions in a collaboration keeps things moving, keeps things fluid, and asking questions when your instinct says NO, helps you to see the situation from a new perspective. You may not necessarily agree with some statements, but instead of disagreeing flatly, keep asking questions and moving forward.

Be humble - allow yourself the freedom of not knowing. What you believe to be real is only your perception. Consider 'what if' and humbly ask questions around those possibilities to see if you might see a new way forward. As individuals, we do not always have all of the answers, together we do.

Be authentic - speak from the heart, be open. If you don't know something, be honest about it and as people identify with YOU, the real you, not a facade or facsimile that you have created of yourself, you will build trust. Trust is the hidden ingredient that facilitates speed in collaboration and allows the project to flow. People find it easier to trust when they feel they are being presented with an authentic and genuine person.

Be vulnerable - you can show you are being authentic when you allow yourself to be vulnerable. Show you are human, point out the error of your ways, empathise with others who are going through what you have been through and you will find yourself aligned with many people who share these experiences.

Failing is powerful - in our society we see failure as a bad thing. What if it were redefined to be a good thing? We learn from our failures. If we never fail, how can we grow? Don't be downhearted by a failure, repurpose it and get back on the horse, stronger, wiser and one step further on your journey.

Work in your genius - no, not the Einstein genius that society considers a freak or unnatural occurrence, but the genius that is you at your best. What are you naturally good at? What is it that you do when time seems to fade away and hours disappear because you are so engrossed? That is you, working in your genius. In a collaboration you need to be aware of what your gift is and own it! For example, why would I be in a collaborative team and let someone else do the content creation - unless it was their thing too? For me, writing is pure joy; I can happily create for hours, as long as I have a purpose behind my content. Don't be part of a collaboration doing something that is hard work for you. The whole point is for everyone to be delivering what they love to do and being complementary to others in the team.

Occasionally, you may have to cross into unknown territory to get the job done (and you can use this as a learning opportunity) and of course, as you grow you may understand and use your genius in different ways, but when you understand how it feels to operate within your genius, you will be empowered to collaborate in a way that creates a bigger impact for everyone involved.

Have you ever been part of a team where you witnessed someone being extraordinary and delivering at an incredible level? Well, that was them in their genius and loving every minute!

Be ready to share - in today's world we often feel that our knowledge is currency and we don't share it because it is hard won, we feel it is our worth. However, in reality, whatever we 'know' that we can sell is already out there on the internet, for free. Keeping everything to ourselves is, actually, counter-intuitive. Sharing what we know is the best way of creating amazing value in a collaborative group. In turn, when others share, it adds value to the group and new initiatives often come from that collaboration.

In my experience, although a collaboration has one objective, when skills, talent, knowledge and alignment all come together, there is usually more than just one outcome, those new ideas or initiatives then develop and have a life of their own - sometimes even bigger than the original goal. That is the magic of collaboration - when all of the elements come together, something wonderful is created that no one could have anticipated.

Have integrity - professing to have integrity and being your word in my experience, is not enough for us fallible humans to follow through. A project requires accountability, and this occurs because the people in the collaboration have integrity. We also need to be able to demonstrate our integrity with actionable accountability as laid out by following the Rules of the Game. More on that to follow.

People will tell you that they have integrity. It means different things to different people, as our monthly *Collaboration Global* meetings have proven in our discussions on this topic. However, I have discovered that some people only demonstrate integrity when it is convenient for them. I have experienced people telling me that they have integrity because they turn up on time for meetings, as they value people's time. Yet the same people frequently cancel meetings to see me at a moment's notice, because *you will understand* when they have double-booked. Yes, I get that I am complicit in this as I allow it to happen, my point being it is human nature to say one thing and occasionally do another. The intention is good, the flesh is weak. It is a part of being human.

Accountability is simply a way of supporting the integrity of the project and the individual.

Context is key and goes hand in hand with integrity as a factor in the success of any project.

If you are fired up about a project, passionate for its fulfilment, you will definitely be in a better position to ensure completion. I have heard people cite that once you have context in a project, in other words *know your why* then taking the action around that context becomes easy, no more procrastination, no more distraction. Well, I beg to differ. In my experience, no matter how strong the *why* there will always be a need for accountability. Consider the overweight, unfit person who has experienced a heart attack and survived and now professes they will adopt a new life of exercise and healthy living. They have a massive *why* - to stay fit and keep the weight off - TO STAY ALIVE! and yet... the weight slowly creeps back on. What causes this? Well, without the integrity of their decision and accountability for at least a few months, to help make their new way of living settle into an ongoing lifestyle, they will often fall back into old unhealthy habits. I'm sure there are exceptions, but we are creatures of habit and the flesh is weak and our inner voice strong.

By making accountability part of your collaborative project, you ensure that each person is supported as they meet their agreed objectives. This is not about the carrot and stick mentality but rather supporting integrity. Committing to an action and being accountable for that action ensures you maintain your integrity. In other words, by utilising accountability you ensure ongoing success.

Some people do not need to be kept accountable as they have integrity, their context is clear, in which case being held accountable is easy for them. They need to lead the way for those who are not blessed with such clear direction and focus, especially if the project is not a passion but is simply utilising their skills.

Accountability can be created through gamification, rewards, asset building, whatever it takes for that group to succeed. This needs to be mutually agreed at the beginning of the project - what works for some won't work for others.

With no accountability, if one person slips, they become the weak link in the chain.

How else does collaboration make you a better person?

It helps you to be empathic, see new viewpoints, push yourself to new heights, discover your own talents by trying them out in a collaborative team, see yourself in a new light. When you are working within a team who are all following the same guidelines, you learn together; about the project, adding new skills to your portfolio, about others, seeing them in a new light and ultimately about yourself, as you identify your limitations and push them to the limit.

Collaboration isn't always easy - we are constantly struggling with the current paradigm of fear, scarcity and competition. In that place, collaborations are often stressful, divisive, unsatisfactory and unhappy places to be. Once there is self-awareness, and the paradigm is acknowledged as one of love, connection and abundance, then joy, inspiration, and success can follow. I know which one I would want to contribute to.

Collaboration In Action

Before you start your next collaboration, can you identify with these characteristics?

- Being authentic
- Allowing vulnerability
- Having integrity and the practice of accountability
- Knowing your genius
- Being empathic
- Being humble
- Seeing failure as opening up possibility
- Being solution focused
- Sharing your knowledge for the benefit of all

Can you identify a time when you demonstrated each of these characteristics? Examine how it made you feel, letting go of negative emotions and connecting to the positive empowering ones.

Not all of these traits are essential for collaboration to take place, but to have experienced these at some point will enable you to connect more powerfully with others in the collaboration and create a fantastic springboard to get working together and deliver amazing results FAST!

Chapter 3

IS THERE ANYTHING STOPPING YOU FROM COLLABORATING?

Have you been in a team, where you are all gung ho, ready to be awesome for yourself and others, you feel inspired by who is in the team, excited by what you will deliver and have a vision for what you will create?

And yet…

It fell apart.

Why the… What the… When did… How did…????

No one put their hands up to say they were responsible for the demise of the project, and yet plenty would have pointed the finger at the person they believed was at fault.

And there lies the first hurdle.

With the best will in the world, and every reason to make it happen, if people in the team cannot take personal responsibility, the cracks will start to show.

Knowing collaboration as I do now has only come from the

personal growth of many failures. Yes, by failing we learn the most, and I am grateful for the failed collaborations that have given me so much knowledge. I now identify myself as a *natural collaborator.*

However, that learning, mine and yours, can only come from being self-aware, as we discussed in the previous chapter.

I have learned to be aware of my own triggers - what sets me off, spikes my defence mechanism and to understand my behaviours - why I do what I do when things go wrong.

Let me elaborate using one of my experiences of a failed collaboration.

A group of business coaches wanted to pool their talents and design a product that would utilise all of their expertise. The idea was amazing, the execution, not so much.

The first meeting as an observer was hilarious, for all the wrong reasons. Each ego took it in turns to take to the front of the room and share their idea on what the product should look like. No acknowledgement of the previous person, no building on what had been said before. Not even saying previous content was of no value, simply ignoring what had been said. As time went on and no plan, outline or strategy was forthcoming, some were getting triggered. (I am not sure whether this was relevant, but there were eight men and me.)

I did not speak to the room, merely observed how they were descending into childish jibes shallowly disguised as humour. Assumptions were made that I would be taking notes - yeah, I know, I raised my eyebrows too.

The day-long meeting came to a close as we summed

up what we had heard, identified some of the tools needed to continue and agreed a date for the next meeting.

A month later, a full-on repeat of the same behaviour, and we got nowhere fast. The idea of self-organising was appealing and, as Don Beck had explained in his study of Spiral Dynamics*,[1] it was an emerging consciousness, a new way of society coming together to organise itself and we had believed we were up to that challenge, hence me stepping back and learning from the group. Despite being quite brilliant in their individual businesses, the idea of self-organising was beyond them.

So I started to make them accountable, set deadlines, put a brief plan together and actions from our meetings. There needed to be someone at the head to guide and build the talent into a productive team.

We got there in the end, but it took almost a year to build the product, test it and create an audience. What we didn't have was honesty, because it then turned out that no one was prepared to step up and market the product. I had anticipated it would be a collaborative effort (oh yes, I can hear you saying it now - don't ASSUME!!) and ultimately, because no one person was coordinating a strategic marketing plan, it never got sold.

What a waste of effort.

All business coaches, and yet not one could or would take the lead. Very good at telling others what to do - the reason they are business coaches!

What lessons can be learnt from this project?

---

1 https://en.wikipedia.org/wiki/Don_Edward_Beck

Sooooo many, in fact, as I learned more about collaboration, it was clear to me which roles we had not established (don't worry, the first three roles will be explained in more detail in future chapters) but let's acknowledge the basics:

1. It needed a *Visionary*- to hold the vision
2. It needed *The Catalyst* - to build the right team
3. It needed the *Driver* - to drive the project forward
4. It needed the agreed rules of the game
5. It needed a strategy - including identifying the market etc.
6. It needed a plan and timeline
7. It could have done without the egos flaring up
8. It needed a marketing plan and agreed collaborative implementation
9. It needed accountability - again not assuming that everyone had enough integrity to do their part
10. It needed more fun

The first three profile roles must be identified in order to expedite the project. Other roles can add weight, but these three are essential to underpin the whole concept.

We will explore more specifically the logistics of how to build a collaborative project in the next section, but I want to illustrate that personality had a large part to play in the downfall of this collaboration.

What was my experience?

I witnessed ego sharing - *this is my best stuff, so you should be grateful.*

I saw people being dismissive of contributions, and dismissive of how much they would contribute because their business took precedence. This mindset in particular was frustrating to me, as we could all potentially have earned substantially from the product being developed, so in effect it was part of their business and not a fanciful sideline.

I witnessed laziness, poor punctuality, being distracted (is it just me who gets annoyed by people being on their phones and then asking the person speaking to repeat themselves?) and, ultimately, the general expectation that everyone else should be running around after them and doing the actual work.

This wasn't the failing of just one person; this was 80% of the room! Sadly, it had a knock-on effect on the people who were originally happy to do the work, and they too, became disillusioned and quickly excused themselves.

What was I responsible for?

Well, I know that I get triggered by male ego, and the bigger the ego the more sarcastic I can become - no, not helpful at all.

I also dug my heels in by refusing to be the sole person to take minutes of the meetings. I did one, but when others didn't step up I wouldn't take up the slack. Stubborn, yes.

I know that I could have given more time to the project, but I allowed my ego to justify it - if they can't be bothered then why should I? Yes, rather childish, I'm not proud to admit it.

At the time, I was probably suffering from imposter syndrome too (not feeling that I was good enough to have a place at the table) and was unlikely to speak out for fear of ridicule. I'm pleased to say, I've now found the cure for that particular problem, in brief, I acknowledge that there will always be someone who knows more than I do and I will always know more than someone else, it doesn't make either of us better than the other. When I see the person standing in front of me as a *Human Being First**[2] then I am no longer intimidated by them. We are all here for a reason.

Judgement forms a large part of failed collaborations. We have our personal historical version of what is good or bad, right or wrong, and with our limited view we make judgements from our belief system. Have you ever caught yourself relaying a conversation you've had and smattering the conclusions you draw with, *I think she thinks…* or, *He didn't say as much, but that is what he was thinking.* In reality, we do not know. We *think* and therefore draw many negative conclusions in order to look good or make ourselves right.

Having escaped this damaging way of looking at relationships, I can understand how easy it is to make up a full soap opera from an encounter with no evidence that that is what they are really thinking. We are all very quick to judge each other. It actually serves no purpose and, indeed, closes down possibility when you *decide* that that is what someone means, instead of taking the effort to find out what they actually do mean.

In my experience with these coaches, I can see that judgement from me, and others, was a major factor in the downfall of the collaboration. Had we been awake to this and were able to allow, instead of judge, we might have been looking at a different outcome.

---

[2] This is one of the core values of *Collaboration Global*

In a collaboration there will be times when you need to allow a situation to play out, to see where it might lead. Being in judgement of individuals or situations is restricting, to both creativity and possibility. When a suggestion is made we can develop a knee-jerk reaction depending on who made the suggestion or what area of the project it is connected to. Our judgement - both good and bad - will cloud the view of how beneficial the suggestion is.

By allowing a suggestion to be fully investigated, you are able to dismiss your judgement and may discover a world of potential opening up to both you and the project.

I know that I am aware of that familiar knee-jerk reaction, it manifests as an intuitive gut wrench that I quieten to ensure I listen to the suggestion without judgement. If I need to forgive someone a previous transgression it might be a good way to dissolve the negative feelings and move on. Or reviewing the suggestion calmly with no axe to grind I can see how it might not be useful to the project. Simply refusing an idea, out of hand, does not serve the project.

Having a heightened awareness of whether I am sitting in judgement or whether I have the capacity to allow from a place of love, forgiveness and gratitude means that more collaborations will succeed. Test your feelings with someone you trust and explore the validity of them. If this is intuition speaking it will shout loud.

When you are looking to collaborate do you jump in with both feet, or are you cautious? Perhaps you have seen a collaboration degenerate and now feel like it is easier to go it alone? If I had allowed the coaches collaboration to colour my judgement, I would have missed out on so many wonderful projects that have happened since. I simply use them all as a learning curve to bigger and better projects, secure in the knowledge that I have built a system, an ideology that will support me going forward. My failings inform my future. I refuse to allow limiting beliefs to be part of my psyche.

Understanding yourself is the first piece of the puzzle to creating incredible collaborations and opportunities. Knowing what triggers you, by being totally honest with yourself and acknowledging where you might have been an idiot, where you got triggered, how you allowed someone to make you feel inferior or demeaned you, not only empowers you for whatever you want to achieve, but will also make you attractive to those who value collaboration as a tool to achieve their dreams. You will be sought out, valued and in demand to make projects come together. Trust me, the people who are self-aware and can collaborate effectively, are relatively few. Understandably so, when you consider the influences that are put upon us - we are not trained by our society to work well with others. By stepping outside of your limiting beliefs, your ego, the internal mind that has to put meaning on everything, you release yourself to see your world in a whole new light. Then collaboration becomes possible and everything you have wanted to achieve with your life becomes possible.

Ideally, it is easier to connect with others who are like you, aligned to your passions, want to make a positive impact on our world and understand the power of collaboration. They can be found anywhere, you simply want to be open to having deeper conversations with people who can feel inspired by your purpose and who are aligned to your values.

This is in part how *Collaboration Global* was born: we kept the conversation going about how powerful collaboration can be when used in the right context and people became attracted to who we were and what we wanted to achieve. They aligned themselves with our mission to Connect, Collaborate, and Grow.

Going solo is tough, but you don't have to do it alone. Imagine what it is like to work with 'grown ups', to be inspired by people who are out to make a difference and who want YOU to be on their team. Understanding collaboration has multiple impacts, for your business, for the people you work with and ultimately for you as a person because of how much you learn about yourself after every project.

Sharing and supporting each other is a much more loving and natural state to be in. It creates a powerful energy that promotes good health, positive vibes that translate to a happy lifestyle. Being around negative, competitive energy serves no one. We are all here to thrive, not to struggle to survive, and by working together in a safe nurturing environment we all get to win.

You may have experienced bad collaborations in the past, don't let them hold you back from being part of beautiful projects in the future, ones that will make you proud. Anything worthwhile is worth working for, and connecting to others who want you to succeed, as much as they want to succeed, is a whole new way of looking at your working life - and beyond!

Collaboration In Action

Spend an hour alone or with a good friend exploring collaborations in the past that did not work out. Being honest with yourself, can you identify why it didn't work, specifically what can you be responsible for?

Did your ego get in the way?

Did you want to take charge and dominate but didn't have permission from the group?

Were you judgemental of the project or people?

Did you suffer imposter syndrome and allow others to take over?

Were you aligned and fully understanding of the context of the project?

What would you do differently?

1. https://en.wikipedia.org/wiki/Don_Edward_Beck

2. This is one of the core values of *Collaboration Global*

Chapter 4

WHAT SORT OF PERSON COLLABORATES?

You are open to the idea of collaboration, you see why it is a powerful tool, you know you can achieve great things and you are ready to move away from some of your current thinking to make collaboration a success. As we've discussed, we need to start with the individual, take the learning into your business to create a successful collaboration and then share your learning with others.

So, what does a collaborator have in their toolbox that means collaborations are more likely to work, and not just work but be massively successful. This is not solely about what you DO in a collaboration but the foundations start with who you are BEING. In other words, who can you BE so that you will create ongoing collaborations?

Self-Awareness

As we have mentioned before being self-aware is the perfect place to start. Do you know yourself? Really understand yourself? Aware that this understanding is actually a lifetime's journey. Have you completed any personal development courses, been on a retreat, spent time delving into your inner psyche? Yes, sometimes all of this sounds a bit woo woo and too much of a stretch - especially for us Brits! Yet once you start, it can become addictive, trust me I've been there! The point is, without some assistance it is almost impossible to search our inner soul to discover why we are who we are and what has shaped our lives to this point. In other words, we don't know what we don't know. Having another person or a group to explore with you, to ask powerful probing questions, to help release previously unseen beliefs and attitudes becomes a powerful tool for you to utilise and will help you to understand others too. All essential to have empowering conversations in a collaboration.

Do you know what triggers your emotions?

What is your go to behaviour when you feel threatened?

How do you handle a temper tantrum - yours or others?

Do you know your values, literally gone through an exercise to identify what is most important to you in this world?

All of these things can be uncovered in a place where you discover yourself through personal development. Whether that is through the likes of Tony Robbins - *Unleash The Power Within*, or via Landmark Education - *Curriculum for Living*, *More To Life*, or one of the very many other courses available to help you understand yourself more, diving in to some self-development even if simply journaling on a regular basis to explore your emotions and picking up a book from the self-help section in the library will pay dividends.

This exploration will uncover all of the little *ways* we might see as charming but are actually hiding a character flaw that is holding us back. Let me give you a personal example.

For years in our house we had an annual BBQ. It started as a celebration for our girls for passing their GCSEs and as the excuses to celebrate escalated, so too did the BBQ. What started as a dozen people popping over, morphed into more than 60+ people and a bit of an event, with their friends and of course, ours too. We all loved it!

What I hadn't realised, was that I became a monster in the run up as I organised it. So much so, that the girls used to conveniently disappear just at the point when I needed their help. They would ring their dad to see if it was *safe* to come home or was mum still in 'that mood'. In my head, I wanted everything to be perfect, but people weren't pitching in with the same fervour I was expecting, and so my anger rose and I became the ultimate martyr, doing everything myself. By the end of the day, I was almost too exhausted to enjoy it.

I spent a weekend at Landmark Education on the Advanced course, where I realised that I was creating the situation (as opposed to all *them others* who were ruining my life - see chapter 1). My *concern* as identified on the course was, *Why won't someone help me?* But when I tuned into my *poor me* behaviour they all knew that nothing they did was good enough, so quickly escaped my wrath by getting out of the house. The joy of the day could have been lost for everyone. When I identified my martyrdom, the coach asked me, *How's that working out for you?*

A blinding flash of the obvious made me see that my behaviour was pushing away the very thing that I wanted.

I needed to change and not *them!* An epiphany!

The weekend at Landmark Education gave me the luxury of time for me. I was able to work through emotions and limiting beliefs. When the realisation came, it was so obvious what I was creating, I was dumbfounded that I couldn't see it before.

We become so entrenched in our beliefs that our mind cannot see another way. I had probably had it pointed out to me a hundred times before, but I wasn't willing or able to listen - then. The difference being that, on the self-development weekend I was working on ME and so I was on the look-out for insights into what makes me angry and why. (As well as what makes me upset, happy, what triggers an argument... and so on.) Going to a deeper level I also learned that nothing *makes* me have any emotions, it is what I was creating for myself. It was an unconscious choice and one that had originated from my childhood. It is like peeling the layers of an onion as we learn how to uncover the origin of our emotions and how to choose a more enlightened approach to our lives.

Spending time learning who you are is the most precious gift you can give yourself. It opens up a box in your mind where you have been hiding things that are too painful to contemplate - your shame, vulnerability, feelings of inadequacy, hate, blame. Dealing with each, one by one, you become brave enough to deal with them and you grow from within.

The more knowledge you have about yourself, the easier it is to collaborate with others. Being open to your own idiosyncrasies helps you see them in others, and you can help others to overcome theirs too.

A couple of weeks later, there was the annual BBQ and I chose to try out my new persona. True to form, both girls found a reason to leave the house and later rang their dad to see if the coast was clear to return. I overheard the conversation, *Not sure what has happened, but she is fine, yeah come back.*

When they returned, they found me happily preparing a salad, music playing, chilled out. They asked if everything had been done and when I replied, *No*, the look on their faces was classic! They asked if they could help and I said, *OK*, and soon we were all preparing food and singing in the kitchen - what a difference! It wasn't perfect, we weren't quite ready when the first people arrived, but that didn't matter, we all had fun taking part and I didn't have to stress and yell to get anything done.

Now it wasn't overnight that I changed, on occasion I could spot where I would normally have automatically gone into martyr mode and been upset that no one was helping. It took time and I had to learn to ask for help. In fact, I still find it hard to ask and my default setting is to say, *No, don't worry I'll do it*, and then feel resentful of the person who was too lazy to help. What I have learnt is that people actually enjoy helping, and (with my attitude) I am preventing them from being useful.

Acknowledge Others

Another facet of being self-aware is to acknowledge others in your life who help you. If you go through life believing you create everything in your life, then you have a massive burden to bear. Others play key parts in our journey and for them to continue to contribute to who we are, it is wise to acknowledge their contributions.

It was Erkan Ali, a previous business partner who introduced me to Landmark Education and I acknowledge his loyalty to this group and his understanding of the power of their courses from his many years in the organisation. Landmark has contributed to my understanding of who I am, whilst still a work in progress, and within every new collaboration I undertake to be open to new learning and greater self-awareness.

It is a life-long journey. No one is ever done, fully cooked. Although I have come across people who say they have done personal development and so don't need to do any more. Warning bells! I don't believe we are ever finished.

I know that, when I surround myself with inspiring, talented and passionate people, I raise my game and become a bigger and better version of myself. Consistently reviewing relationships, by what I contribute and how we interact, helps me to define what I want for myself and others. A stagnant relationship serves no one.

A suggested glossary of personal development coaches and courses are included at the back of the book, plus of course our own Academy at *Collaboration Global* provides a wealth of resources.

Forgiveness

One of the biggest things to hold back your self-development is an inability to forgive those that have wronged you. Not simply people on a collaborative team, but further afield. If you hold a grudge or any unforgiveness in your heart, that will (directly or indirectly) be stunting your ability to grow. Being able to grow is imperative in any collaboration. Possibly a relationship in your life has broken down and you still nurse an anger or grudge that occupies your thoughts. A schoolteacher may have made your life miserable or you were bullied at work, you may have physically moved on, but have you emotionally let it go?

I have seen this manifest in eating disorders, sleep deprivation, anxiety states and dormant anger to name but a few. Again, how does genuine trust and an authentic relationship develop with this background of underlying negative states?

Collaboration Global member Benn Abdy-Collins sums up the power of forgiveness in this quote:

'Forgiveness is freeing; it frees energy, it empowers love, it engages creativity and it enables bridges to span chasms of feelings, emotions and the gaps we can all fall into.'

Know Your Genius

Do you know what you are good at? No, not just good but really awesome? Indeed, what is your genius, your specialism, you in your flow?

By this I don't mean what are your qualifications, what certificates do you hold and what experience do you have, I mean what is the stuff you LOVE, that gives you a BUZZ, that you would do even if you didn't get paid to do it?

When you identify what that is, you become a key player in a collaboration. Personally, I don't want to be working with a team unless I know everyone is 100% aware of what makes them awesome, what they are a genius at. It puts a whole new perspective on the project and makes it an almost spiritual experience - yes, even a simple marketing project. When you witness a team coming together, aligned with their why, owning their individual space, respecting others' genius and creating with integrity, the final completion of a project is often an emotional experience.

What do you need to do in order to understand and identify your genius? Don't be shy, what do you LOVE to do and why are you so good at it?

It is usually an innate gift that has been nurtured and developed, and maybe you even now take it for granted. Own it and let people know that is your thing, imagine if you never did all those things you see as chores and only did the things you see as a joy.

Quite often, we see the things we are genius at as common, everyday things and make the assumption that everyone can do them as easily as we can. I was one of those people. I thought it was easy to network for business, to connect people who are useful to each other, to share my ideas on their business and help them see new ways to make more money. Surely everyone does that, don't they?

It wasn't until I was on a course with about 50 other people and I became known as a connector, that it slowly dawned on me that not everyone could do it. In fact, it became clear that I was the only one in the room who appeared to have this 'gift'. It was a revelation to me.

Now I realise that is not my only gift, and that the easiest way for me to identify the others is to look at what I find easy and love to do. I ask myself: *if I had to do one thing for the rest of my life, what would that be? Why do I love it and who does it help?* Generally, what I come up with is a key component to a collaboration and a space I know I can own.

Be A Good Listener

How many times do you see people listening with the intent to respond to what you are saying, rather than listening with the intent to understand? The most powerful honour you can give someone is to listen, truly listen to what they are saying.

In our fast-paced society, I see people use conversations as a tag game of one-upmanship, trumping a story, denying validity, undermining value. I am sure you have experienced not being heard, and it feels disempowering, frustrating and hurtful. If there is no listening, you feel ignored, irrelevant and unnecessary. Not exactly conducive to a productive collaboration.

Listening is a skill that requires practice. Spend time listening to your children - really listening, and see how quickly the relationship blossoms. In fact, take any relationship that is feeling tired, stuck in a rut, not what it might be, and simply spend the next week listening deeply to your conversations with that person, be open to what they are saying, and see what happens.

An example of how powerfully listening can have a profound effect on a relationship is one that I see often with parents of teenagers. This can be extrapolated to many other family relationships. I get frustrated that society has created a picture of teenagers as stroppy, hormonal, disrespectful and argumentative. This is totally unnecessary if we as parents spend time listening to them. Not relating to them as our children, or seeing them as a toddler having a tantrum, but as an individual who is experiencing change and is uncertain of the future. Listen to them with an intent to understand, not chastise or demean. Listen to them as human beings with valid concerns, even if we consider them inconsequential, they are real to them. I promise you the relationship you have with them will not be anything like we have been led to believe. We have allowed ourselves the famous get out clause of, *Well they're teenagers, what can you do?* This is ridiculous! It absolves us of our responsibility and makes an excuse available for poor parenting. I am not saying that being a parent is not the toughest job in the world, but we are doing ourselves and our children a disservice by succumbing to this ridiculous idea that every child when they hit 13 will be difficult to manage. They are *difficult* in exactly the way you would be difficult if you were not being heard. If no one listened. In exactly the same way as marriages break down, because there was no proper communication and the love was allowed to die. In any relationship, family, friend, colleague - all will be enhanced when you listen and allow them time to be *heard, acknowledged* and *valued.*

Yes, there will always be exceptions, but simply try it for yourself, try listening powerfully in a key relationship you have and see how much closer you become, how richer the relationship will be. In the same vein, if you are not being heard and a relationship is suffering because of your resentment, ask that person to spend time listening to you.

Listen without a need to put anything right, no request to change, or even understand, simply to listen.

If there is someone in a collaborative team who doesn't understand the power of listening, then they may not be right for your team, but it is never too late to teach them.

Be Curious

If we constantly look at what already is, we restrict ourselves from what might be.

On our journey in *Collaboration Global* we have constantly come across people who tell us we should be doing it this way and not that way - because that is what you are *supposed to do*. We have people who say, *I have done this for the last 30 years, so you "should" do it too.* Often these are good ideas and can be a solution to the problem. However, we believe that if we stay curious, dare to be different, be open to the weird and wonderful, then something incredible can emerge.

The *Collaboration Global* community have acknowledged a group of behaviours that create a buoyant and positive outcome for a collaboration. We list them as *Behaviours of Collaboration* - how to behave within the community and subsequent collaborations and indeed life in general. It is not an exhaustive list, I am sure you will find some of your own. This list can be found at the back of this book alongside suggested Mindset. One of these *Behaviours of Collaboration* is to Be Curious which we liken it to a child's wonder at the world. Sadly, we all too often lose that wonder and work from *what is.* This limits us in our understanding and closes off our minds to possibility. Every good collaboration focuses on solutions, constantly asking questions without a need for a definitive answer. If there is no right or wrong, then there are usually a myriad of solutions where we get to pick the best fit.

Collaboration requires a mind that is open and ready to consider the ridiculous and the sublime. It was not that long ago that online banking was considered ridiculous, or even buying an item from a stranger online left us feeling ill at ease. Now it is commonplace and completely normal.

Someone somewhere had to buck the trend in the beginning to get the idea off the ground.

Great collaborations hold the space for curiosity and the 'what if' conversation. That is how genius can escape the confines of doing what has always been done to create infinite possibilities.

Trust

As a collaborative team grows together, it develops a sixth sense, and the trust that is integral to the success of the project comes naturally. With experience we learn to trust each others' judgement, integrity, and genius, which allows our curiosity to go a little wild. In short, trust becomes the strong core of the group relationship.

This cannot be manufactured. It doesn't happen overnight. It is created with time, as each member of the team demonstrates they are trustworthy, it is a process that cannot be rushed. However, if the team comes together for more projects in the future, the trust is instantaneous and becomes a bond that is hard to break.

Trust will allow a project to go further and create bigger outcomes because of the safe space created for each member.

Ever play a team sport?

When I used to play netball, I knew and trusted my team. We were reliable, polished, proud and pretty much unstoppable.

When I was asked to sub for another team, it was a different story. I didn't know who was the safe pair of hands, I wasn't sure of the best shooter to pass to, I didn't know who was the fittest or fastest - who could I trust?

It takes time to develop trust, but a collaborative team without trust will devolve into cooperation. What is the difference? What does cooperation look like?

Cooperation can work, but generally there is a leader telling people what to do, what is required. People do what they are asked and get a job done. Which in itself is fine.

In a collaboration people want to go above and beyond, they want to show off how good they are, they are having fun with each other, the team becomes a close unit who grow from each other, bounce ideas into the ring, pick up suggestions and run with them, tackle obstacles together and support each other to success. The collaboration becomes an activity that is worthy of their lives. They are proud of the result and feel valued for their effort. They find joy in their work and often put in more time on the project because it is not seen as, or doesn't feel like, work.

These are some of the essential ingredients of a good collaboration. Often, they are not available at the beginning of a collaboration and evolve as the group start working together. An awareness of each element can be shared at the beginning of the project, so people are on the lookout for how they can acquire them.

Even people who are not known for their listening ability can learn its value and can be helped to build their awareness around it, whilst on the project.

Some of these elements take practice - we don't all need to be proficient on day one. However, we do need to know that by the end of the project we will have learnt and be able to demonstrate them. As a result, each person will have an in-depth knowledge of their genius as well as the genius of others in the group, will be a skilled listener, have demonstrated integrity, been fully accountable, shown their ability to be curious and think outside of the box.

Moving forward, when you experience a collaboration with others who are self-aware you will be able to identify how all of these skills, plus your own self-awareness, has had a knock-on effect on relationships both inside and outside of the project. A more fully developed and self-aware person is a huge asset to the next collaboration and the next. As you grow in your ability and each collaboration there will come a time when you can teach these skills to others and Pay It Forward #PiF, more about that in Part 3.

Collaboration In Action

The list above is not exhaustive when describing a good collaborator.

List the traits YOU possess that you believe would make you good at collaborating, not the specific skills you have, not things you DO, instead focus on your characteristics that would support a good collaboration. Such as 'good listener' 'insightful' 'optimist' 'adventurous'

And explain why you think they would aid the success of a collaboration.

Who would you want in your team?

Step 2

Your Best Business -
Thinking you alone have all the answers to growing your business is lunacy!

Collaboration helps to build a lasting, viable, sustainable business.

Chapter 5

TIME FOR NEXT LEVEL THINKING

From a purely practical level, collaboration in your business, when done successfully, will make it grow. That might be growth in prospects or profit, it might give you access to more specialists, or strengthen your weaker areas, and it could even give you more time for a better quality of life. What's not to love?

So why don't more people do it? Why do we not have every small business focusing on collaboration in order to be bigger or at least appear bigger? Can it be because people love doing everything in their business by themselves?

In my experience as a business coach, most people struggle on, alone because they have either tried collaboration and were stung, or don't know how to go about collaboration in the first place.

So, first of all, let's explore the benefits of collaborating with someone in your business.

Leverage

If you have a fabulous product but no track record, it makes sense to partner up with an established brand plus someone who will be willing to utilise their database and - all three end up smelling of roses. It is an easy first step into collaboration. The alternative is to develop your own brand (which could potentially take years) and build your own following (which could also take years). Not that you would partner up with just anyone, you want to know that you are aligned, share a vision and will be good for each other beyond the initial project.

The ideal scenario, if you do your homework first, is that you enjoy the process so much, that you all work within your genius, that you love what you do and ultimately create something that none of you saw coming. Working together to offer an asset will build each of you up and benefit all, especially your customers.

A Bigger Team

How many times have you wanted to know something and needed a sounding board? Maybe, you wished you had a member of staff who could take the pressure off you, or someone who had a different skill set so you could enhance your offering?

When my previous business partner and I first got together, it was predominantly to support each other in our separate businesses. Although on paper we delivered the same thing, in reality we had very different skills and could support a client in different ways. By working with a client in a collaborative way, we were able to offer them a more dynamic approach.

Although our businesses were separate, we often would come together to help a client utilising our differing skills. Having someone there to bounce ideas off, who understood the vision and was willing to share skills and knowledge, was invaluable. Being part of something bigger made us up our game too. We learnt from each other and the client got the best of both of us.

I realised I also missed being part of a team. I liked the camaraderie of sharing ideas, someone to tell me I'd had a genius idea, someone to debrief with after a session. Being part of something bigger made me feel accepted, wanted, and gave me a sense of belonging.

Greater Talent - Share Skills

On a purely practical level, in a collaboration you get to share skillsets.

I know my strengths and will happily identify my weaknesses - I am in awe of someone who knows their way around a spreadsheet. We can offer reasons for and suggestions to develop our weaknesses, but when all is said and done, I do not want to learn how to do the split testing analysis of a marketing campaign, I just want to write the words.

We all have our talents, and I appreciate my limitations in both time and desire to learn something new. However, when you have an ideal balance of collaborators (described in the next chapters) the pressure is indeed taken away from having to be the omnipotent *Being* in your business.

Reach More People

We are all obsessed with data in today's world, and exactly how many people we can reach has grown at an incredible pace. However, just because they *Like* you on Facebook does not mean they want to do business with you. In a collaboration we pool our communities and endorse each other to get a greater reach.

Some people utilise Referral Marketing or build Strategic Partnerships, both useful strategies to employ, but these are very different dynamics from a pure collaboration. Generally, these are seen as transactional arrangements, whereas a collaboration has the ability to build lasting relationships that develop loyalty and trust.

How does this occur?

By spending time building alignment, valuing a common culture, working to a shared vision and respecting each others' genius invariably builds the relationship, so that each member of the team is more than happy to spread the word, to share to their communities.*[3] We value each others' contribution and offers of help. Have you had that conversation where you feel you are so aligned, you have just met your new best friend? Instinctively, you want to help them and share their mission. It happens naturally, and with an understanding of true collaboration you have a greater awareness of how to build on that initial alignment and create solid foundations going forward.

[3] NB this is hopefully obvious that you do not email someone else's database. They contact their loyal customers with a suggestion that might be of benefit to them. May GDPR and common sense prevail.

Greater Profit

As your business grows, you often find that the type of client you attract grows with you. Therefore the rates of pay per hour usually grows. The more you are in demand the more you are able to charge for your services.

Working in a collaboration where you can be perceived as a bigger organisation, doing what you love, with people who are aligned, doing what they love, it stands to reason that you will build a level of TRUST that ultimately will save you time and money. Stephen M.R. Covey tells us in his book *The Speed of Trust* how powerful and profitable trust can be in any business agreement. Collaborations that follow the *Collaboration Global* culture, (love, connection, and abundance) will undoubtedly build trust among the group, and so the usual elements of a business arrangement, although still adhered to, are probably not seen as quite so necessary because of the level of trust. According to Covey, both time and money are saved when you go into business with someone you trust.

Help More People

Part of why we collaborate is to undoubtedly help more people. The bigger the project, the more people will be impacted by the outcome. We have seen many collaborations started and objectives set, yet when they reached completion there were outcomes achieved that benefited in ways that no one anticipated, often for people outside of the project.

I assume, like a scientific experiment, there are always knock-on effects, or happy accidents, that often become bigger than the original purpose.

Ultimately, we want to see millions of people benefit from the collaborations that they are involved in, as well as from the collaborations of others. There is a beautiful opportunity to take the learning from each and every collaboration and share that with others for the benefit of everyone, both those going into similar circumstances and for those who are not even aware of the information, there needs to be a *Pay it Forward* philosophy to every collaboration to extract every ounce of value from the mini communities that are created at the beginning of each and every collaboration. If this is a place of Love, Connection, and Abundance, then every collaboration has a duty to continue living outside of the original context.

Don't panic, this isn't an onerous task, it generally happens naturally, but sometimes we need to be nudged to ensure the learning is captured.

As an example, one collaboration I was part of, to be awarded the ISO (International Standards Organisation) in Working Collaborative Relationships 44001, was so profound that the auditor acknowledged that our community was not just ticking the boxes of the audit, but was demonstrating that we were creating it in every every area of the organisation. He wanted to use us as a case study so that others might benefit from our practice. We had not anticipated that outcome, but the fact that our practice could now inform others was an unintended outcome of our collaboration.

More Fun And Someone To Share The Journey With

Life can be tough. Being a solopreneur in business can be exhausting. It's even worse if you have a business partner or partners and the relationship is fractured - that can be the loneliest place on the planet.

If you spend time working on a collaborative team, this often positively affects the whole department or office and you can see massive benefits. For a start, coming to work isn't a chore, it becomes fun. Imagine if you never dreaded Sunday evening because Monday morning was following? That is what it could be like, when your business is part of a collaborative organisation, once you get the groundwork done.

Fancy that?

Well, what is stopping you?

Shall I write the list for you? I can hear you saying it already:

- Once bitten - been there and it wasn't pretty.
- They steal my intellectual property.
- They steal my clients.
- It's too much like hard work.
- It's too expensive when it goes wrong.
- Better the devil you know.
- Staying small is less risk.
- Staying small is easier.

What is the one common denominator in those statements?

Each screams to me of someone who is living in fear.

Fear of making a mistake, fear of getting it wrong, fear of failure.

What if we could take that fear away - make it vanish?!

It is possible. You simply look at your life in a new way, be open to creating a new culture, choosing to be a new YOU!

What do you get by staying the same?

Well you can say you were right. Then what?

You can stay playing small - how would that achieve your life dreams?

You can keep your intellectual property - what if no one wants it?

You can keep your clients - even the ones who don't pay, cause you problems, aren't grateful?

Choose

What we want to achieve by collaboration is not the old way of working. It isn't the old way of BEING. It is our natural state, the state we have forgotten because our world teaches us to look out for number one, to be in survival mode and compete against the rest. For whatever reason, we no longer see the people around us as our support mechanism, but rather as competition waiting to take advantage of us.

We must look with fresh eyes and see our world for what it truly is - a place of Love, Connection, and Abundance.

It takes a while to practice and feel at home with this new way of being, but when we get the hang of it our world returns to us in full technicolour. This is the world I live in; where people talk to me on the Tube; where I leave my purse in a shop and someone takes it to the cashier and it is returned with every penny still in it; where I have a flat tyre and someone stops in the cold and rain and helps me change it. A beautiful world filled with incredible, beautiful, kind, loving, caring human beings.

Do you want to live in my world?

It really is simple.

Choose.

You do this, as we said in Part 1 by working on your self development and understanding that you can take radical responsibility for your life. We do this on a daily basis through a variety of daily responses, everyone is different. By being aware of the distinctions in your life - how you view your past, your present and your future you will begin to welcome all collaborations. That is why we hold regular meetings for our members as a place to practice all of the distinctions and mindsets for collaborative success.

Collaboration In Action

Identify what is holding you back from a potential collaboration.

In two sentences say why collaboration will enhance your business or place of work.

Describe who you need to BE to create a successful collaboration.

Chapter 6

WHO DO YOU WANT IN YOUR TEAM?

Collaborative Profiles

The Big 3 - is all you need to start:

- The Visionary - to build the picture
- The Catalyst - to build the team
- The Driver - to make it happen

Having researched and worked on what makes a good collaboration over the past few years, and indeed learning from success and failure, I have now identified 12 profiles of collaborative characteristics that makes the right projects flow and come to fruition. Having said that, if there are only three people in your team, then the profiles in this chapter are enough to get the job done. However, if you have a bigger team you can allocate each role for clarity and ease of working within a larger group.

Before you do that, you need to set up the *Rules of the Game* a.k.a *Be More Pirate* from the book of the same name as described by Sam Conniffe Allende where he refers to the Golden Age of pirating between 1680 and 1730.

A member of the *Collaboration Global* community provided us with a brilliant presentation about how to *Be More Pirate*, taken from the book and concluded that all collaborations would benefit from creating a Collaboration Code in the same way Pirates adhered to their Pirate Code.

This meant that at the beginning of every collaboration the assembled team would consider and share; values, methods of communication and accountability, time scales, integrity, limiting beliefs, personal triggers, mindfulness, process, tracking, genius, collaboration profiles and access to vulnerability, and much more. In short, an exploratory session to lay all the cards on the table and choose a way of being that would suit everyone in the team. Always better to have your say before any tension is felt and make yourself heard before the project adds additional stress to the situation.

This would be different for every collaboration, as everyone would be bringing different talents to the table - and different idiosyncrasies. However over time it is not remarkable that many of the same values and behaviours would be part of the code.

It's a great way to have an open discussion about what's really important to everyone. It is not just about establishing shared values, but about how they are expressed in behaviours and actions. For example, we can all agree about respecting each other, but have different ideas about what that means. For one person, arriving late for meetings is a sign of a lack of respect for the others, but of no consequence to another, who gets really annoyed if people thoughtlessly copy them in on all emails and messages. Debating what do and don't make the *Rules of the Game* brings these often subtle differences of opinion to the surface and allows them to be acknowledged and resolved up front.

It's also proof that this is a safe space to have open and honest conversations and to resolve differences and address difficult issues.

Remember, you are just agreeing the rules for this voyage of this collaboration, not for all eternity. This impermanence enables people to be more flexible about things and not get stuck taking a stand on something relatively inconsequential. You may hate doing things a particular way but if everyone else wants it that way, you can live with it for this collaboration.

Finding a phrase that embodies the whole project also helps to establish unity and reminds everyone of the Code. KISS *Keep It Simple Sunshine* is also important, it should be easily memorable and not simply a list of Dos and Don'ts.

Creating your Pirate Code gets everyone on the same page at the beginning and gives an agreed set of standards by which to measure behaviour. If someone is not sticking to the Code, it is much easier to point out their non-compliance than to personally criticise their behaviour. It's based on your shared values and so it's much less contentious.

It's also great fun and that sense of play and irreverence is just what you need to make your collaboration a creative, joyful and productive experience for everyone concerned.

The pirates really had a disproportionate impact on the world, punching above their weight and creating long-term change. They didn't just reject the rules and the norms of their society, they replaced them with better ones and created the type of society that they wanted - fair, open and equal. At the time, in the late 1700s, aboard a pirate ship was the only place in their society where a black man could be truly free and a woman could really be an equal.

They even established a proto-republic at Nassau in the Bahamas, a pirate paradise on dry land. They really broke new ground and upset the establishment, rewriting the rules about what was possible. Isn't that exactly what we need today? Isn't that what we need collaboration for?

The pirates were seen as such a threat by the establishment with their heretical ideas about freedom, democracy and mutuality that the Royal Navy eventually ruthlessly suppressed them. Their ideas, though, did not die and were influential in the French and American revolutions that followed. In the UK, they inspired the rise of mutual (or friendly) societies, the establishment of trade unions and the cooperative movement.

Be more pirate and change the world, like the pirates did.

A great start to any collaboration is to set these ground rules a.k.a The Pirate Code. The team starts with no preconceived idea on what they 'should' be doing. The first meeting is to share what they enjoy when working together, such as: is banter required, can you eat on the job, will poor punctuality be accepted, etc. This meeting will also establish what people are good at, what they enjoy (not always the same thing) and what are their hidden ninja skills? Even in a busy office, where roles are already established, it is a good exercise to go through so that no one gets stuck doing what they hate and feels resentful of from the off.

This is also the time to check your ego and leave it outside the room. Agree there is no right or wrong and that possibilities are endless. Any boundaries required should also be set now. For example, I do not particularly like swearing in a business meeting, or actually anywhere. It is a quirk I have, so I ask people to hold back. I prefer them to use a wider vocabulary. Maybe you think that is unnecessary, but on occasion my colleagues have been known to bring their children to a meeting, and sadly some people aren't used to censoring their own language and swear in front of them. Call me old fashioned, I just don't like it.

Whatever might raise your hackles, now is the time to mention it. See those who are in full agreement, spot the ones who are already opposed to you - it might take more time for you to become aligned, or more effort to ensure differences are not a barrier.

It is these ground rules that need to be verbalised, you don't have to agree with them but understanding them, why people have these *quirks*, can smooth the path to a more harmonious relationship.

Now you have an open space where creativity can flourish. Remembering there is no right or wrong and ensuring a solution-focused environment establishes a creative no-holds-barred space where ideas and genius lives.

Now you have a bunch of people who are excited by the project, have an idea of the outcome they want to create, collectively and individually, and are ready to make a name for themselves through the delivery of excellence. I'm excited for them, this in some way is the best part - the beginning, everything fresh, when imagination can run riot.

Whoa hold on there, don't we need someone in charge? Someone to keep control, to manage everyone, to keep to time, deliver goals, keep to budget? Well yes... and no.

Let me explain.

In my previous book, *Making of a Movement* I explain more fully the conditioning we all go through in our society to conform, which in turn has clouded our views on what it means to work together. What I and our *Collaboration Global* community advocate is that all of the *rules* (or what Vishen Lakhiani of Mind Valley would call the *Brules* aka *Bullshit Rules*) have held us to account and stifled our creativity and productivity. The best way to create transformational outcomes is to get rid of the conventional rules and set up our own guidelines for optimal results - hence the first meeting to set up the *Rules of the Game* a.k.a *Be More Pirate*. Setting up expectations and identifying where we best fit into the team will save hours of heartache later.

Within this first session, you also identify the 'Collaborative Profiles' and these will give the *leader* role, which changes depending on the need at the time. When everyone is aware of the potential profiles, as described in the following chapters, they then know who they can defer to for decisions and guidance at each part of the project.

Then the fun begins.

The Visionary - To Build The Picture

One of the most important people in any collaboration is *The Visionary*. They hold the vision for what is possible, they see the outcome, they identify the need and can paint the picture of what the collaboration will achieve. I cannot express more emphatically the importance of *The Visionary*. They may not be in the collaboration at the end but without them there is nothing to grow from. It is the role of *The Visionary* to hold the vision for others. It is very easy for us to get pulled off-piste and end up delivering a solution that doesn't actually fulfil the brief or falls short of the initial vision. Don't expect The Visionary to know the details, they expect others to work that out for them.

They also aren't the ones who will hold the project together 'til the bitter end - they will be off looking at other bright shiny objects. However, they will be passionate about the vision and instil this in others, plus have a very clear context of *why* it is worth pursuing.

They will be a solid base from which to climb, helping the team to realise the vision even when it doesn't always seem clear.

Without a *Visionary* there is no purpose, no context, no reason for being. They create the emotional charge to bring the project to fruition.

The Catalyst - To Build The Team

Next we need to find *The Catalyst*, which is the role I played as we set up our first community. You may remember a YouTube phenomenon known as *The Lone Nut - Leadership Lessons* from Derek Sivers, where a crazy dancing guy was filmed at a festival and within three minutes had demonstrated the formation of a movement. This was our experience. A Visionary on his own is just a *Lone Nut*, but once joined by *The Catalyst*, he has validity and soon they generate a small following who resonate with the mission.

At Collaboration Global our ***mission*** *is to establish a* *global community, online and through local groups in towns and cities around the world, that provides the conditions for people to come together, collaborate and realise their individual and collective potential.*

Initially, my role as *The Catalyst* was to put in place ways that our mission could be realised, in the form of our group meetings. This soon grew into our online publication and the podcast, eventually growing into our platform and The Collaborator Academy. We even embraced the establishment and acquired the ISO 44001 certification in Working Collaborative Relationships. Small collaborations sprung up around us and my role developed into the Community Catalyst, ensuring people connected on a deep and meaningful level and our members were experiencing transformations in their personal and business lives. Connecting people was something that I had not previously acknowledged was indeed part of my genius. I see immediately where collaborations are possible and intentionally put people together where I see complementary talents and shared markets. Even when I see people struggling, I feel duty bound on a human level to share with them who they should talk to in order to get more support or knowledge for their needs. So, every *Visionary* requires a *Catalyst* to get their vision off the ground.

The Driver - To Make It Happen

Next, we require a *Driver.*

How many times have you seen great ideas struggle and die for the want of someone to drive it forward?

This person is your accountability buddy for the team. They ensure meetings are ended with action points, that previous action points are completed, integrity is upheld, people keep their word and living *below the line* by giving excuses, blame or denial just isn't an option. In short, *The Driver* delivers a professional team who bond even more because they aren't watching or waiting for others to fail, they are simply delivering their genius for the benefit of the team. *The Driver* also has a sense of urgency, as a brilliant project manager they have high standards of themselves and expect that of others.

One of the things we have noticed with any of our collaborations is that no matter how high the expectation or intention for a good outcome, we are all human and inevitably someone fails to deliver. This can have a huge impact on the outcome of the project, but at the very least it impacts the morale of the team. It is very disheartening if you are burning the midnight oil, are passionate about the project and give your all, only to discover someone else doesn't have the same commitment and cannot even be bothered to complete their agreed task. All sorts of ramifications come into play - do they have any integrity, are they committed to the project, are they passionate about the outcome, do they care for what they are doing, are they truly working in their genius or out to *look good*? Ultimately is it that they are simply lazy and shouldn't be on the team?

Finding out any of these possibilities sooner rather than later is the role of *The Driver.* In short, they help to make the team accountable. It helps to distinguish the genuine team player who had a delivery issue from the person who doesn't deserve a place on the team.

With one person responsible for overseeing the accountability of each member, the rest are reassured that everyone is pulling in the same direction.

With the top three profiles in place, you can get your project off the ground. As in any new business, there will be multi-tasking along the way, so perhaps *The Driver* or *Visionary* may also take on another of the roles until more people join the team. The next two chapters describe an ideal scenario where we have all of the roles in place, remembering that each person accepts the role that best fits their genius. That way the whole team are doing what they love and have a certain autonomy over their domain.

Collaboration In Action

Who do you know who can fill these roles?

Who do you already love working with - what role would they be perfect for?

Start to build your perfect collaborative team.

Chapter 7

COMPLETING THE COLLABORATIVE DREAM TEAM

The Special Six

- The Strategist - to make a plan
- The Technician - to develop the idea
- The Tweaker - to make it better
- The Salesman - to share with the world
- The Multiplier - to build scale
- The Monitor - to keep things moving

The Visionary and *Catalys*t from the previous chapter are very good at right brain, big picture thinking, but ask them to create a plan and they will immediately look around for someone else to do the detail. They will happily give *The Strategist* the overall concept, talk neverendingly about the context of why it should happen, but ask them to deliver a strategy of how, and they will struggle. This can sometimes be done by *The Driver*, especially if there are only three people working together, but again, the delivery will come from a place of frustration. They all know it has to be done, but none of them are naturally capable.

The Strategist - To Make A Plan

The person who will relish this role is *The Strategist*. They love the minutiae of planning out the long-term strategy, seeing how it can be improved on week by week and watching it come to fruition. A *Strategis*t is not someone who will necessarily be dealing with the tactics or game play, instead they will be overseeing how every element fits together and how this will impact the final result.

The Technician - To Develop The Idea

This is the person who brings 21st century thinking to the project. It is not merely someone who will develop a website, it is the person who understands the strategy, sees the long-term vision, understands the capability of tech and offers new solutions to the potential seen and unseen issues along the way.

For us within *Collaboration Global* this is Kay Westrap, always working with us on the boundaries of our financial capabilities and yet still enabling us to reach beyond what we thought was possible. She gave us joined up thinking, old school values matched with tech solutions. It was our vision and culture that brought Kay into our world and she has been one of our strongest contributors and allies. An essential in our team, who we couldn't afford, but who has aligned herself with our mission and is now someone we couldn't do without.

The Tweaker - To Make It Better

This person is tasked with looking at every action, every implementation and asking *why*. So often we are so immersed in a project or even our whole business and we cannot see the wood for the trees. We often do things simply because we always have, there is no consideration whether it is still valid.

In one business, I worked with a director who was very attached to his filing system, which had been in place for years. I struggled to move him away from this model, until I pointed out that every day he was traipsing across the office to file an invoice and when extrapolated into *time spent*, we saw that he was wasting about three weeks a year because of this old way of working. Once we equated that into £££s, he was desperate to update the system. If I had not been there to *tweak* many of his inherent systems, he would still be wearing out the carpet today.

Potentially everyone could be a *Tweaker*, but I find when the responsibility is given to one person, they are more likely to own it and make it their own. Please do not confuse this with the person who feels they are being helpful by pointing out your errors, or who picks holes in every new venture. We need to see pitfalls, but if we considered every pitfall, I doubt the Wright brothers would ever have got that first plane off the ground.

Having awareness around the project is the same as having self-awareness, it opens up possibility, having someone purposefully consider why you are doing every action or task gives you the opportunity to ask why. Ultimately, we do not know what we do not know and ensuring you have someone overseeing and improving when and where they can provides a tight ship (back to the pirate analogy again

The Salesman - To Share With The World (And By Salesman I Mean Human)

There is no point having the best idea, product or service and it being the best kept secret. The person who is overseeing how the product or service gets to market is not necessarily the one who does the closing conversation. This person oversees how the message gets through to the market, how each member of the team sees their responsibility and ensures everyone has the correct tools to shout to the world about the product.

Yes, one person may be naturally talented to sell or to market, so they will probably be *The Salesman*, but not necessarily. We often separate sales and marketing and indeed they are very different roles, but a collaborative *Salesman* in this scenario, ensures that those with the talent share their knowledge with the team so that everyone learns how to sell the product. I have often heard it said that marketing makes the phone ring and sales closes the deal. Having that person in your team responsible for the world knowing about you means they ensure everyone within the sales/marketing team are all on message. They all understand the desired outcome and work together to ensure they get the results. They are not separate; they need each other and the other profiles to create the right result. In many companies, sales and marketing are divided and appear to be in competition with each other. If collaboration is your aim, in order to access leverage for your business, then internal competition serves no one.

The Salesman works closely with *The Visionary* to distil the message and *The Catalyst* to ensure it spreads to the right market.

The Multiplier - To Build Scale

An initial vision holds little detail. When we talk of being global, it is the role of *The Multiplier* to spot how this can happen. Seeing how systems can be put in place to ensure consistency of delivery, performance and most important culture and message. A business that isn't scalable holds little value. Like buying a house, it is generally considered a good buy if you can demonstrate where the value can be added - an extension, additional bedroom etc. In business, people willing to invest are looking to see how it will scale.

Now some businesses will not want to capture a global market and so have no need to show where scalability exists. However, putting systems in place is a practice every business should undertake; it underpins continual improvements, prevents repeated mistakes, creates innovation potential and ultimately offers an exit strategy. Having someone in your collaborative team who is overseeing this is invaluable.

The Monitor - To Keep Things Moving

This profile is, on the surface the same as *The Driver*, but coming from a different perspective. *The Driver* keeps integrity high, *The Monitor* oversees that genius doesn't get out of hand. They are tasked with creating and nurturing a timeline for the project. Getting agreements in place and ensuring the completion in a timely fashion. We understand that when a collaborative group comes together with all aspects of the team, with self-awareness of the collaborators and a vision in place, then time can become part of a parallel universe. By this I mean that *The Monitor* oversees the genius of the rest of the team and, as part of their own genius and ensures that the main project comes to fruition. However, this might involve allowing new off shoots to become budding projects in themselves, but will not allow these *bright shiny objects* to overshadow the main vision. When you are in your genius and ideas keep springing forth, it is very easy to lose sight of the big picture and, potentially, the main project can become side lined. *The Monitor* ensures this will not happen, whilst keeping the new ideas flourishing alongside the main vision.

All of these profiles will undoubtedly be doing the doing too. In other words, *The Strategist* might also be a web developer, or *The Driver* might be creating content, whilst *The Monitor* might be overseeing the finances. However, if these roles are not specified and expectations laid out, then the project might find itself in difficulty.

In *Collaboration Global* these roles have grown organically, people have stepped up to take them on naturally. This is how we have learned how good collaborations work, what happens as projects progress taking the good stuff into new projects, while also seeing why some collaborations have not flourished.

Yes, some people are not sufficiently self-aware to be part of a collaborative project, or sometimes they have a level of self-awareness but are still unable to leave their ego at the door.

Imagine if someone tells you your integrity is in question - no one likes that. Yet we need to have it flagged up if we are damaging the project. Not surprisingly, when people know there is someone in the role of Driver, then integrity ceases to be an issue.

By having these roles in place, we are giving everyone the best start to ensure success.

We are only human, we live in a society where many people survive by *getting away with it* and *looking good*. When you are part of a powerful collaboration you rise above your limiting beliefs, define your new sense of being, choose to be the best you can be and by doing that there is a new level to who you are. Collaboration gives you the opportunity to be your best self, to reach your full potential. Not because the boss tells you to, not because you will be paid a vast amount of money to get the job done, but because YOU are delivering your genius for the benefit of YOU, your collaborative team, and your clients. Pulling together to make a difference gives everyone an incredible feeling of self-worth, but more importantly of belonging, too.

Collaboration In Action

Identify what is important in your life and bring that to your collaborations.

Identify what makes you angry and bring that passion to your projects. The passion of wanting to make a difference - to help others, to create a better world…

Think about who you need to be so that you create the change you want to see.

Chapter 8

IN AN IDEAL WORLD...

If the business owner isn't on board, preferably playing their part, then the team will falter. They also have to see the value in the final three profiles:

- The Nurturer - to look after the team
- The Financer - to make the numbers add up
- The Finisher - to make it sparkle

Collaborations are, by definition, full of people and people have needs. Therefore, it stands to reason the team should have someone responsible for looking out for the needs of the collaborators: a gentle hand to support, an ear to listen without recriminations, a place to go when the genius isn't appearing. We all have dark days. Whether it is life taking over or the headspace conversation becoming too loud, we all need someone to be there for us. Maybe you already have that *Go To* person in your group of friends, quite often it is a different person for a different need. What if there was a member of the team who had no one they felt they could talk to?

The Nurturer - To Look After The Team

They are there to spot warning signs, to offer help, to listen and to help each collaborator make choices that will support them. I learnt the hard way that there is huge value in having someone you can turn to.

In the early days of BeCollaboration (the forerunner to *Collaboration Global*) my mother died. Not unexpectedly, but having lost my father too it made a huge impact on me. In my life I had been taught to keep my head down, suck it up, work hard and the hurt will pass. I did and it didn't. I ended up three months later (having worked long hours for seven days a week, trying to block out my grief) passing out cold for several minutes. When revived I escaped to bed, where I slept soundly for almost 20 hours. This was a warning sign to me and to my family that I was not coping.

Had my nature been to ask for help, had I been able to speak with someone, had people not assumed I was fine, maybe my mini breakdown would not have happened.

I then went on a long journey to recover and began asking for support - something that back then had been impossible to do. If you imagine that I had been brought up in a family where my maternal grandmother had coped single-handedly with the death of her husband while she had three children under seven years of age, the youngest only six weeks old, then heard that World War II had broken out, you can imagine how I was used to hearing how we have to *get on with it.*

Limiting beliefs can hold us back in all sorts of ways.

That is why I believe every collaborative team requires at least one person to hold the torch for those who are in need of support. With proven strategies and tools to share, they will enable the person can deal with their issues.

If I had been part of a collaborative team at that point, I know I would have been dropping the balls I was juggling, trying to keep up appearances while crumbling inside. If there had been a known person - *The Nurturer*, who was there to help, there to listen, there to spot me struggling - I am sure I would not have been allowed to push myself that hard and end up hitting the wall.

Life can often throw us a curve ball, and knowing we have someone looking out for all of us doesn't mean that others don't have to, it signals to everyone that we need to be kind, we need to watch for unusual behaviour, we need to be there for each other. *The Nurturer* will be tuned in to the mood, the energy of the group and will be able to step into a dispute or concern before it escalates. There is always someone you can go to, in confidence, to get you back on track - no recriminations, no opinion, but a listening ear and a different perspective to support you in the team and in your growth.

The Financer - To Make The Numbers Add Up

In some of my successful collaborations, most of the people were not concerned with the money. They don't know how much they will get, they aren't concerned with how much they can generate, they care little for how much the project will cost - totally crazy right?

Generally, people in this state of mind are having too much fun, have no concern for the project to end and there is little urgency to get the job done.

This is part of my learning when we review projects, if there is no one to keep their finger on the pulse as far as the finance is concerned, then often the rest of the team can miss a trick. Whilst working from an abundance mindset there is no need to be concerned, and for many, thinking about a budget can put restrictions on their genius, their creativity, however, when someone has the responsibility to oversee the budget, and has a goal to aim for as far as the remuneration and profit is concerned, then the others can create without hindrance. There is nothing more frustrating than when an amazing project comes to fruition and there is next to no profit in it. It becomes unsustainable and that outcome serves no one. Money is not an evil to be avoided, it is a tool we can use as a measure of fair exchange.

Society has developed an attitude around money that generally does not serve us. If you have read Robert T Kiyosaki's book *Rich Dad Poor Dad*, you will understand how differing attitudes around money can have a profound effect on the outcome of your life.

The secret for me is to generate recurring revenue and not be at the mercy of debt. Easier said than done, but I know people every day who cannot remove themselves from the addictive impulse to buy designer label goods or be seen to have money-guzzling hobbies. I find it hard to admire someone's Mercedes on the drive when I know they don't have enough money to pay what they owe to other people. One friend I have has coined (unintended pun) the acronym OPM *Other People's Money*, that she identifies as someone who is happy to splash the cash when it belongs to someone else. I think we might all know someone like that.

In a collaborative team it is possible for someone who might be susceptible to a bit of OPM spending to be frivolous with the cash. Rather than oversee the funds by committee and expect everyone else to agree to a spend, *The Financer* is the agreed person to oversee any spending. This helps everyone to be free of the burden, whilst keeping the person susceptible to spending OPM in check.

Money can also be a very emotive subject. In a collaboration we have to provide a win/win/win at every level, and everyone should be prepared to work at this until each person is happy. If just one person feels they are not being valued as a result of their financial agreement, then either they must be supported to understand how the calculation came about or the agreement reviewed. *The Financer* is the person who can logically, and without prejudice ensure the money flows in the right direction.

The Finisher - To Make It Sparkle

Finally, the role that takes little effect until the very end of the project - the person responsible for ensuring the finished result will make everyone proud. They review the project, see how a fresh pair of eyes can hone it and often improve on the original vision, and see which part might be continued above and beyond the original remit.

What we have discovered, with many collaborations, is that when three or more people combine their genius something occurs that none of them had anticipated. It is this revelation that *The Finisher* often spots.

Simple things like, for example, when I wrote the *Making of a Movement* book, it had been through editing and proofreading by the team but it wasn't until it got to Mitch

Herber of Catalyst Design, who was typesetting and printing the book for us, that he suggested we should have an inlay of photographs of our sessions and some of the personalities of the community. It was a lovely suggestion and, since we started selling the books, that is a comment that regularly comes back to us, how much people enjoy seeing us at our meetings and social occasions. People get in touch because the photos made us so accessible, they felt like they knew us already. A perfect finishing touch, Mitch had not been aware that this was part of his genius, as he regularly spots improvements his clients could make to their print work. So simple, yet he adds value on a regular basis.

The Finisher is also looking to acknowledge the team, spot their combined talents to see how they worked together and whether any magic can be replicated on another project. *The Finisher* comes into the project when it is 75% complete, supports where they can and suggests additions in the final stages. They understand the make-up and dynamics of the team and identify what isn't working - maybe someone has taken on a role that isn't a good fit for them, a fresh pair of eyes will spot this even when those working in it haven't.

The Finisher also liaises with *The Visionary* to complete the circle.

Now if this collaborative team is in a business then ideally the business owner would have a part to play. Not necessarily an active everyday role, but at least taking one of the profile roles to ensure they understand the culture of the group and can contribute to the dynamics of the project. Being part of the collaborative experience will enable them to connect with their workforce at a deeper level and give them a greater understanding of what a great team looks like as well as what might be produced in other areas of the business. The team will also see a more inclusive leader who is not afraid to bond with their staff and build deeper relationships with them. This in turn develops loyalty from the team and generates indirectly greater profits for the business.

The 12 profiles are seen like the actors in a play, they arrive on stage at varying times, tell their part of the story and leave only to return to take their bow at the end. Their collaborative team has created the magic that tells their story.

Collaboration In Action

If you own a business where might your workforce be collaborating?

If you are employed, where might a collaboration support the company?

How might you as the business owner create a better culture through collaboration?

Chapter 9

A WORD OF WARNING

Now you have all of the players, you can start the game, but a word of warning - there is no right way to create a successful collaboration!

In the same way that there is no one diet that will work for everyone, there is no 100% guaranteed method of perfecting collaboration. Sorry, we are all human and life can get in the way. That is not to say that if you prepare yourself with what might go wrong, aim to cover all the bases in this book and you practice the culture of collaboration, you are pretty much on to a winner. But just in case all is not going smoothly, here are some suggestions for what might be holding you up.

There are many things that can get in the way of a great collaboration. The obvious one is the lack of self-awareness by the members of the collaboration. That is not to say they cannot learn along the way, but they need to be open minded, and perhaps more importantly open hearted, to understand the nuances of collaboration. Someone walking into the team with an ego that they can't leave behind will probably not last long.

When our learned behaviour causes us to revert to our old ways it is usually because the paradigm of fear, scarcity and competition has kicked in. Having experienced a society predicated on those emotions, we easily slip into the limiting belief that we have to look after number one. In a collaboration where we extol love, connection and abundance you can see how this juxtaposition will rankle with some. If they don't get it, don't understand generosity of nature, sharing ideas and gifting solutions, then you will find conflict in some form - it is almost inevitable.

If there is an assumption of integrity yet no one is appointed for accountability, the finger of blame can be pointed and immediately the energy will flow from *we* to *them and us.* As you can imagine, this is not conducive to good collaboration. Any division within the group is the first sign that true collaboration has broken down. Not irreparable but troublesome, nonetheless.

Generally, the person who has been blamed will become defensive and feel they are required to move the blame to others to level the playing field. If people do not feel able to own up to a mistake or inability to complete actions, they will fabricate a story to save face, or cover their failings. This often triggers emotions from childhood that result in behaviour that is truculent, unreasonable and unhelpful. It is very hard to come back to a fully supportive team when this has occurred.

Trust is a fundamental part of any good collaboration and when this is lost, for whatever reason, it is virtually impossible to bring the project back on track. Everyone will instinctively revert to their known comfort zone and begin protecting them self from potential psychological attack. The opportunity for sharing without fear, demonstrating abundance and whole heartedly supporting each other is going to be a miracle to retrieve.

If the problem comes from just one person, then there is hope that it can be salvaged providing they are replaced. Hopefully with full explanation, so they can learn from the experience.

As with most things in life, money can get in the way of a smooth-running collaboration, or more accurately the lack of it. Most people have a story around money - never got enough, money is the root of all evil, money doesn't bring happiness, etc. etc. They bring this with them, and I have once seen this attitude stall a great collaboration before it had even begun:

I spent an entire afternoon with two people who, between them, could not agree on the appropriate cut of the profits and how they would be distributed between our fledgling team. This was before the model had been decided, the strategy agreed, and roles allocated. Nothing like putting the cart before the horse. The collaboration floundered almost immediately as this was their main focus. They weren't considering the people they would be helping, what their genius was or how they would deliver the content. Ultimately it was their egos that failed them, but it was the money conversation that flagged up the warning signals for me.

Ironically, they both thought they had a money-spinner on their hands, but neither were prepared to invest their own cash into the project. There was no sharing, caring environment to bask in, but one of 'I deserve a bigger cut because of my expertise'. In the end no one gained a penny.

This leads neatly into the ultimate bad collaboration when someone is totally self-interested in the project, in other words, WIIFM (*What's In It For Me?*).

I have had the misfortune of working with narcissistic personalities who were totally out for number one. On the surface they said all of the right things and yet my gut was feeling the warning signs. I listened with my head and not my heart and stumbled into a world of angst, upset, unkindness and unfairness. I tried to rationalise my decision and stayed with a project for six months, but ended up losing money on the collaboration and more shocking for me, I lost sleep too! A lesson for me was that I needed to pay attention to my intuition and be prepared to say *no!* For me, a great collaboration is not all about the end goal, but the journey we all go on to achieve it. I want to work with people I respect, who show they trust me, who earn my trust and who I know love and appreciate me. A great collaborative team doesn't feel like going to *work*, is a joy every day and certainly shouldn't give you sleepless nights!

I used to say I loved being part of a team - as long as I was leading it! Now, from all of my research into collaboration and my experiences of great collaborations, I find that this is the least successful way to operate. Imagine; being solely responsible, having to make decisions on minor issues, managing the budget even from afar, creating and building the culture of the group, or hoping they gel, get on OK, don't argue too much... In a team and in our current climate it is all too easy to use the person at the top as the one to blame. Blame for over running on time, running out of money, achieving a poor outcome, even for poor performance when others make mistakes, or don't deliver. Now that isn't to say all of these things can't happen in a collaboration, but when it is a true collaboration if they occur there is someone to take responsibility, someone to have ownership and someone to be accountable.

All people in a collaboration are equal, they own their integrity and deliver their genius - not because they have been told to, not because they are being paid to, but because they are operating at their highest level in their genius and therefore are loving being part of it. If they fail, it is a collaborative fail, which often signifies a closer step to success. I believe that a collaborative team is always looking for the win/win/win. Win for the client, win for the team and win for the organisation/world where unexpected value is paid forward to a wider community.

Now I'm sure there will be people considering that it isn't always possible to create a win. Is that because we do not spend time looking for it? What if we were trained to look for it? Stephen R Covey who wrote the famous book *The 7 Habits of Highly Successful People* wrote about one habit being Win/Win and believed it was possible to work towards a solution on ANY subject.

"When one side benefits more than the other, that's a win-lose situation. To the winner it might look like success for a while, but in the long run, it breeds resentment and distrust."

Dr Stephen R. Covey

As time has evolved in our community I am confident that a win/win can be created from any situation, we have to commit to searching for it, often simply from a place of love. That is when you make amazing discoveries.

When my teenage daughter was frantically yelling that she had lost a piece of homework, I asked her to show me how she had looked for it, she walked into her room and with a dramatic sweep of her arms gestured, *See! It's not ANYWHERE!!!!*

I slowly followed her and noticed, not for the first time, the state of the room and asked if she had actually moved anything to really, really look for it?

Her exasperation and frantic expression suggested not,

so, for the sake of a quiet life I set to searching. I moved an item of clothing strewn across the floor and discovered said homework. Relief flooded the room.

Do most of us look for a solution in that way? We can do A or B, we can buy or sell, we can say yes or no. When in fact we need to search harder, do some heavy lifting, make some effort to find a solution.

When I work with my clients, they often have a scenario where they only see two or at most three options. Once we have finished our session, we will have accumulated upwards of 20 different options for them to contemplate.

Our fast-paced world is not geared up for the 5,000 piece jigsaw, (does anyone have time anymore?), but sometimes the conversation we have while slowly finding the blue bits gives us opportunities to discover new solutions. We have to work at it, and when we do, a solution is always available to us.

Collaboration In Action

Look at areas of your life now where collaboration is happening - are any of these collaboration blockers occurring? Can you save it before it is too late?

Look at a suffering relationship in your life where there may not be a collaboration, but where systemic win is not part of the focus. How might you create that win/win and improve that relationship?

Who do you know who is self-sabotaging their potential because of their ego getting in the way? Can you help them?

Chapter 10

WHAT HAPPENS WHEN IT FALLS APART?

As much as I believe that every collaboration can be successful, there are inevitably ones that don't turn out the way you would expect them to. That doesn't mean they fail; they just don't end in the place you had planned them to go.

An example of this was my business relationship with the co-founder of BeCollaboration. We started with the same values, on the same mission, with a vision to make the world a better place. Over time we became obsessed by the possibility of how much impact and potential our new community could create. It had all the hallmarks of success, I had no reason to think it would become impotent.

Bear in mind we weren't fully aware of the nuances of collaboration in the early days, and so no ground rules were set up, profiles weren't considered and expected outcomes were not established.

We began building BeCollaboration (as you can read in my book *Making of a Movement*) in 2013 and by 2016 cracks were beginning to show. We didn't want to acknowledge it, but we were beginning to grow apart, instead of being on the same page we were agreeing to disagree. Nothing wrong with that, in itself, we were regularly checking in with our values, but the message we wanted to share was coming from two different perspectives and confusing the listener. I worked hard to see where he was coming from and checked in with people in our community if they felt in tune with his views. Slowly and almost imperceptibly we drifted apart.

People change.

As the distance increased, we stopped checking in, our values invariably changed and the friendship suffered. Don't get me wrong, in all of the time this was happening we were striving to bring it back to what we had first created, but circumstances impinged on what we were able to give and the future together became bleak. There was no upset, no anger, no vitriol, simply deep sadness and some frustration that we couldn't bring it back on track.

By the end of 2018, I was chasing a dream, and as I entered 2019, I knew I had to step up and lead our community. Over the course of 2019, we worked to see what might be salvageable, but ultimately with me leading the community it was morphing into something he didn't want. What we had created was no longer his dream. He had to move on.

That takes nothing away from the genius that had built the partnership and the lessons we both learned. Had we not started BeCollaboration I wouldn't have specifically researched collaboration, wouldn't have pursued my own personal development with such rigour, practiced coming out of my comfort zone, developed wider communities, reconnected to my spirituality, built my emotional intelligence and identified the specific distinctions required for successful collaborations. I also would not have started our podcast 'Being Human - Hidden Depths' or developed and published our online publication 'The Quest' or learnt the plethora of software applications that we now use to run the business. I also would not have been blessed with The Dream Team who help me to look after the organisation today.

This is just the tip of the iceberg. There are many, many, hidden benefits and lessons to be learnt that I am still uncovering.

My biggest learning from this experience?

That not everyone is capable of collaborating.

That not every collaboration can end with the intended outcome. That doesn't mean it isn't ultimately successful, just not what we had originally envisioned.

That we have to be present to the unexpected success we do achieve.

That you need to have the basic ground rules in place to stand a fighting chance of success.

If it doesn't work out, forgive yourself - you cannot control every element of a collaboration. The very nature of it means people have to be responsible for their own outcome.

There is always learning to be taken from every collaboration.

Setting expectations would have saved time, if they are not being met you can make a decision to move away sooner rather than later.

Don't waste time thinking it will get better when the evidence before you says otherwise.

A quick way to know for yourself if it is time to move away from the collaboration is to ask this question - *are you happy?* Answer without the if only, maybe, because, perhaps… just check in with your gut, your intuition. *Do you feel 100% happy with the way it is going?* If the answer is *no*, then it doesn't mean the death knell of the collaboration, but it does mean you continue with more stringent resolves, putting in place defined expected outcomes and timelines. Then check in with yourself every week - and if you can record no ongoing positive growth, then the time has come to say goodbye.

Looking back, I continued for 18 months when I should have made the choice to move away much sooner. By staying I probably did more damage in the long run.

Ultimately, the biggest thing I learned from this collaboration not working out was that my vision is still strong, I am still passionate about helping people to collaborate and reach their full potential. Now, some months on, I can see it is the best thing that could have happened, I am no longer in mourning for the lost partnership, I am celebrating new possibility with full acknowledgement of what our time together created. It is a massive win/win/win as we both move away in different directions and my logical brain, emotional intelligence and intuitive self all concur that it was my best choice, for me and him, and the community.

Collaboration In Action

Are you in a collaboration now that feels a bit clunky?

Have you got your *Rules of the Game* in place?

Check your values are still aligned.

Give yourself some space to connect with your intuition and ask the ultimate question, *Are you happy?*

Put some measurements in place and review - then choose.

Chapter 11

WHAT DOES AWESOME LOOK LIKE?

Well, we have covered some of the pitfalls, by no means all of them, so now is the time to look forward to when you have built an amazing team for your collaboration and it is flowing, what does that look and feel like?

What I have experienced when I am working with people who are loving what they are doing and who are delivering work that blows me away, is that we are all feeling joy. It is a joy to go to work, it is a joy to be in their presence, it is a joy to deliver my best self to support them. I have no fear of ridicule, no concern that I won't be appreciated, no feeling of imposter syndrome or worry that I need to keep on top of everything - because I already am.

The energy in the team is positive, full of fun and there is an excitement to be creating together. There is a strong acknowledgement of respect for each other, and reassurance that we are working with professional like-minded and like hearted people. Working within the *Collaboration Global* culture of love, connection and abundance there is an understanding of how we speak and listen to each other.

What I love about a collaboration that has all of these ingredients is that I can relax, I can simply BE me. I don't have to fight to be heard, I don't feel the need to justify myself or prove my worth - or worse be seen as one of the boys. In the past, I have experienced the macho, ego driven culture of a male environment and had to change who I was to fit in, to 'be one of the gang'. This might have been due to my inexperience and insecurity at the time but nevertheless I didn't feel able to be myself, I had to put on the mask, laugh at sexist jokes and pretend I wasn't offended in order to fit in.

Did I deliver my best work? Definitely not, I was in survival mode, doing more than I needed to in order to be accepted, and resenting the culture that didn't encourage me to speak out, be brave, make mistakes or try something new. It was a toxic and debilitating environment and I couldn't wait to leave. I was a talented and innovative woman who was capable of transforming a whole department into an efficient and productive environment. Instead, I left and felt justified in leaving chaos in my wake - yes, very childish, but I felt they had it coming.

Fortunately, the *#MeToo* movement is making organisations more aware of these situations and so hopefully less people are suffering this sort of treatment. Although individually they were lovely people, collectively the culture was laddish and based around what they could get away with. It is very easy for one person to sway the team - for good or bad.

So, when collaboration works it is something to applaud, to relish, to review and identify why it worked, who made it possible and how it can be replicated.

When a collaboration works it deepens the relationships of those in the team, people feel connected because they supported each other, they created something that they were proud of and they had fun doing it. Often, they will want more opportunities to work together and they proactively look for innovative, new projects. These relationships can also create a loyalty to the company, because if they leave they will have to find another person who gets them, who clicks with them, will they be able to replicate the success in a new team? The power of a successful collaboration leaves ripples of good outcomes, not just from the work completed, but also from the new opportunities that arise from the genius within the team. Their joy of working together on the collaboration brings the feel good factor into every area of the business that is affected by the project and the team.

Likewise, a collaboration that doesn't bring joy will also spread ripples of negativity.

A good collaborative team may fail at the project, but they will see this as a stepping stone to success. Possibility will still be ignited and eventually success will follow. If the team and culture have not been set up for success, then negativity will be pervasive. Relationships may falter and future projects will be approached with caution. When working under this veil of expectation with potentially limiting beliefs of why a previous project went wrong, it becomes almost impossible to find the joy and creative dynamic of a successful collaboration.

The difference between a team that has experienced a great collaboration and one that has suffered at the hands of a 'see how you go' mentality is the difference between night and day. Emotions run deep when working with others. When it works and you know why it works, you can replicate it and discover the magic again and again. When it doesn't work, it often leaves behind emotions that are hard to let go of. It takes work to remove grudges and deep-seated frustration and anger. What happens, as in my case, is that often you lose members of the team - they walk away.

Ultimately, when you take more time to set up the collaboration for success within a business, you are ensuring your team delivers above and beyond even their expectations. This in turn will translate into more profit, loyal staff, a creative dynamic, a recognisable feel good factor in the business that your clients will be attracted to and a better place to be for everyone. Your business will build a reputation for a great workplace, where everyone wants to connect and be part of the magic.

A classic example of this is the Seattle Fish Market which, on paper, is not the best environment to work in - early morning starts, cold, smelly and very hard physical work. Yet it is now a world-famous tourist attraction because of the collaborative team that set a mission to make it world famous. They now love what they do, have fun, build a huge fan base and are loyal to the company.

What has sprung from their original intention is a whole new business; they now travel the US to share their FISH philosophy of running a successful company.

You never know where the collaborative potential will take you.

Having a great culture in your company is paramount, add that to a collaborative team using the principles set out here and watch the magic happen. As we have discovered the possibilities are endless.

Collaboration In Action

Start with a small collaboration following these guidelines and experience the magic.

Get the foundations right first - don't rush it.

Diarise the results, good and bad, so you can be wiser next time. Every collaboration is different and every person is different; both can improve.

Step 3

Time To Pay It Forward

**Creating a better planet -
if our world is set on self-destruct,
how can collaboration
make a difference?**

Chapter 12

LET THE COLLABORATIVE GENIE OUT OF THE BOTTLE

Now we have a better understanding of what makes a powerful collaboration, isn't it our responsibility to share that with others?

Let's take this one step further, what if...

- Political parties collaborated - Jacinda Ardern has a focus on policies with Well-Being at their heart, more of that please
- Governments collaborated - can't be worse than they are doing at the moment
- Religions collaborated - advocating love
- Organisations reviewed their operations and began to collaborate for the benefit of everyone - it can be done
- Children are taught how to be solution focused (note the difference - not problem solving, solution-seeking)
- Human Being First - people stop differentiating on needless criteria like race, gender or age
- Every organisation starts with the culture - make kindness a priority, as we have seen during the age of COVID-19

Learning about myself is one thing, growing my business is another, saving and transforming our world is... well, on a whole other level!!!

We are so conditioned to look at our societies and accept the status quo, feeling impotent and unable to make an impact, that it is only the rare individual that takes on the establishment. In the USA there is a phrase to keep constituents in their place - *You can't fight City Hall*. We are not supposed to rebel or go against the norm and I get it, in a civilized society we wouldn't have to step *out of line*. So, what do we do if we feel the lunatics are running the asylum?

And we don't want to fight.

We don't want a violent revolution, as is happening in many parts of the world right now.

Do we put up with the growing need for food banks, the growing homeless problem and the inner-city gang warfare that means young teenagers feel a need to carry knives to protect themselves?

We need some form of change, but I don't believe revolution is the way to go.

What is required is for ordinary people, like you and I, not to play the game; not to be a consumer for the sake of consumption, to consider the planet as we heat our homes and eat our food, to offset our carbon footprint when we can, and question everything we have been taught.

We need to be consistently kind to one another, help our fellow humans, share our knowledge, define our values and remind each other that we are here for a purpose. Define that purpose, and lead your life with your mission to make a difference. We have our personal mission but eventually we all realise that we are here for the rest of humanity, to help each other to flourish.

Most importantly, we need to connect with other people who are committed to being part of a humanity where everyone thrives, no one is in poverty and everyone can have a safe place to call home. Yes, this can be perceived as Utopia and, indeed, it might seem unattainable at this moment in time, but please for one moment, just one, take time out to reflect on what that world might be like to be part of.

Imagine a world where you can walk home and there is no one sleeping in a doorway.

Consider a world where children are educated in subjects that they are fascinated by, in places that stimulate their imagination and support their natural curiosity.

Contemplate a day when the news on television is all about the good stuff of life and advertising is on request. Where race, gender, age, are not things that define us. Money is abolished and power is held by the many and not the few.

I can hear the incredulity in your voice as you read this text. Does that voice sound something like this?

It can never happen.

She is living in cloud cuckoo land.

Not a realistic bone in her body.

I get it, I am dreaming of a future world that works for everyone. Yet for me, this isn't entirely a dream. From my small experience in the *Collaboration Global* community, I have found people who already live their lives in this way. Already share their wealth, support others, share their knowledge and love unconditionally. What if we gathered more people who lived and shared their lives in such a way in order to demonstrate what it means to be in a culture of Love, Connection and Abundance?

What would that look like?

What if….

Governments adopted this strategy? There are already signs that this is possible. Jacinda Ardern, Prime Minister of New Zealand, has initiated a *well-being budget:*

'We're embedding that notion of making decisions that aren't just about growth for growth's sake, but how are our people faring?

How is their overall well-being and their mental health? How is our environment doing? These are the measures that will give us a true measure of our success.'

The world has moved on and the old systems are not serving our needs. Capitalism and its measures of financial growth to define success are showing the cracks. It doesn't serve and we now see that infinite growth is damaging our planet and in turn fracturing communities and isolating individuals. It takes people like Ardern to step out and offer new solutions. When other governments see the impact her new policies have, focusing on well-being, hopefully they will follow suit.

Is it a sweeping statement to say that governments, as we know from our own debacle over Brexit, are more interested in battling for power than serving the common good? That is not to say that some politicians aren't focused on helping their fellow man, but we see again and again that once they are thrown into the parliamentary system, they soon become hardened and join the pack, or become disheartened and leave. This is what we experience in our everyday lives. Generally, animals hunt in packs.

Have you ever worked in an office where you initially feel the culture is a bit different to what you are used to? Maybe they have some sharp banter. On closer inspection you realise the banter is generally targeted at one or two people in particular, who smile and seem to take it well, even though it can be quite cruel - funny on occasion, but still a bit mean. You realise that if you don't laugh and join in, you will soon become a target for the hilarity. So, you comply. For a quiet life, to fit in, be one of the crowd, to be accepted, you join in. Doesn't matter, does it…?

For you maybe not, but for those targeted it can be having untold emotional consequences. We cannot see mental illness in the same way we can a broken bone. Your conscience is a barometer for your actions. If you feel it is being unkind, then you pretty much know that it is. Don't be the person that fits in with a culture that doesn't make everyone feel great. Stand up and be counted. In the same way if we are OK over in the West, we cannot ignore the country that is being ruled by a cruel dictator.

We are all ONE! We are all joined and when we stand together, we can overcome all adversity. We have to be the change we want to see and lead the way. Easier to do when you aren't sticking your neck out all on your own. There has always been strength in numbers, and as part of *Collaboration Global* you will find many people who agree with your values and are willing to stand by your side.

Imagine a huge bucket of negativity. Every time you move away from Love, move away from Kindness, give up on Possibility, you add a drop to the negative bucket.

YOU are responsible for filling it up.

Now, next to it imagine a huge bucket of positivity. Every time you make a stand, support someone's needs, share your wealth, share your love, you are filling up that bucket. We are all responsible for living a life that will have a positive impact on others, a systemic win for you AND me. Yes, it is difficult to stand up and be counted, but if we don't do it for smaller incidences when only our feelings can be hurt, how can we expect another to do it when it means a life is at stake?

Easier said than done I know. Which is why you need to hang out with like-minded people who will build you up emotionally, provide you with emotional armour so you can make that stand and be impervious to the response of negativity.

This *revolution* can start in local *Collaboration Global* sessions as well as globally online, where you can practice the culture of Love, Connection and Abundance. Spread the word, build the movement and demonstrate the power of collaboration when it comes from the right values and culture. Practicing it with others demonstrates the power of transforming into a new paradigm. Teaching people how to operate in a community, focusing on being selfless instead of selfish is the way forward.

We are unaware of the subliminal messages that we are fed daily that keep us in fear. Every news bulletin would have us believe the world is overflowing with wicked people, when, in reality, they are a tiny minority. Sadly, some of them rule countries, but still in the minority.

'The only thing necessary for the triumph of evil is for good men to do nothing.'

John Stuart Mill

By starting with ground floor communities which naturally want to help each other we begin to build the foundations of a society that functions for the benefit of everyone. This can then filter upwards and affect larger and larger communities and ultimately redefine how we govern our society. Can we all agree that our political system is not performing as it could? Ego is the common denominator of our MPs as they bay and gesticulate in Parliament. How can anyone have respect for a system that was created hundreds of years ago and was built to serve the male upper classes? It doesn't fit. Most importantly it preaches a them or us, right or wrong, in or our mentality which simply isn't realistic.

'If you always do what you've always done,

you always get what you always got.'

Attributed to many

It is time in our world of mass knowledge, in the technology age, at a time when we can access a computer on our wrist and more, to get back to some basics. We are HUMAN BEINGS FIRST. When we connect to our innate BEING our intuition, our conscious mind, we can access a new way forward. This can only happen if we stop looking at the problem and start to look for solutions. Not simply problem solving, that limits us, we need to develop a solution-focused, collaborative mindset to discover a hundred new ways of being, to create a new way for our society to live, grow and thrive. Let's find solutions that fit the majority of good, kind people and not the minority with money and power.

We can develop guidelines for governments, religions, schools and societies to follow, which support every individual to become the best they can. No one gets left behind. Everyone is supported and there is no need to live in fear or be lonely. Being alone is fine, if that is what you choose. Ultimately, we want people to be able to choose their life, and not have it dictated to them by others purely because they have lost their human rights or are caught in a community that doesn't pull for their greatness. Modern day slavery is shocking, but we allow it to continue because someone somewhere does nothing. Another drip into the negative bucket.

I am not professing to eradicate all evil from our planet - although it's a powerful ambition to have on my vision board. It probably won't happen in my lifetime (although remember I am an eternal optimist) but what if we could get so far, what if we could make a difference to some, as though their world has turned upside down and they can now experience love, connection and abundance.

Wouldn't you like to be part of that?

I love that at every *Collaboration Global* meeting without fail, someone is impacted by what they have learnt. Someone acknowledges that one of our members has made a difference to their lives and our guests comment on the palpable energy of love in the room. We are already making a difference to our members as they experience a new way of being and many comment that it is their monthly fix of Feel Good. It is not only a place of the warm fuzzy feelings, it also challenges and supports people as they venture out of their comfort zone and transform into their best selves. It can be messy, it can generate emotions of failure, inadequacy and not good enough. This is all in the individual's past conditioning and they are now taught to see that failure is a growing experience, there is no wrong, they are always good enough. When they want to grow, there is usually a barrier for them to overcome and with the help of others they can. No one has to tackle life's challenges alone.

We are learning in this space how our world could look.

And it looks *amazing!*

We don't have all of the answers, no one does, but we have found a possible way of making our world a better place to be.

Chapter 13

IF NOTHING CHANGES?

According to the *experts* (see references at the end of the book) if we continue this trajectory, we will be inviting not only environmental disaster but also personal loss, too. It would appear we are on a pathway to self-destruct. We become more and more isolated and our mental well-being suffers. Chasing the money god as we eschew our faith in our spiritual gods means we rely only on the physical and do not support our emotional well-being.

We forget that we are connected consciously as a human race.

In this century, we have seen a rise in the teaching of spiritual health. The gap between religions has on occasion been emphasized in extremism, acts of violence and, again, the media has done nothing to dispel the anger that this creates. Rather than bringing us together - allowing worship that does not denigrate any faction of society, that brings people together in love and not hate, these horrific acts have in some quarters, been set out as a symbol of a whole religious following, which is simply untrue.

In the *Collaboration Global* culture our core value is Human Being first. We illustrate that we don't have any consideration of whether you are white, black, green or blue, young, old, tall, short, fat, thin, rich or poor, gay or straight male, female, gender neutral etc. etc. etc. you are a human being FIRST and that qualifies you to be loved and to explore the possibility of collaboration.

When considering how our consciousness operates, we can see negative influences everywhere. Evidence of the paradigm we live in can be seen especially in all forms of media, we are continually fed a diet of fear, scarcity and competition. The results of this can be seen all around us. In social media we have 'trolls', in TV soap operas there are shocking story lines, our newspapers have sensational headlines and our news reporters don't even speak normally, their tone is of continual shock and disbelief - which, when you actually listen to the words being said, is ridiculously comical.

If we consider how this affects the average member of the public, I despair. A brief example; - I was at a party one evening and catching up with some people I hadn't seen for more than twenty years. We kept to safe topics and the story of Meghan and Harry leaving their royal duties came up. Personally, I was only aware of the outline story of two young people no longer wanting to be hounded by the press and choosing to raise their children abroad - perfectly reasonable to me. Yet the people I spoke to were using words and phrases like *disgusting*, *wicked* and *I hate her*. They had seen in the popular press, articles that they were taking as fact and were forming opinions about the situation that enraged them and they were physically disturbed by those emotions.

On the Dawkins[4] scale of emotions, they were lowering the bar considerably.

When I slowly explained to them that we do not know those things to be true, and asked even if they were, how does it affect us personally, and why should they feel so venomous to the couple, they eventually climbed down from their principled stance and saw it from a new perspective. They are still entitled to their opinion of the situation, but have an opinion without the vitriol that perpetuates ill-health and can have a knock-on effect on their personal relationships.

It takes an effort to help those who do not even understand the concept of collective consciousness. That is why I believe *Collaboration Global* and all it teaches needs to be accessible to as many people as possible, so they can realise they do not have to live in this perpetual state of feeling upset, angry or offended.

Dr David R. Hawkins illustrates in his book *Power vs. Force* that by coming together and raising our emotional vibration we can positively impact the world.

With coronavirus we appear to have an opportunity to reverse this negativity as we come together as a society and applaud our essential workers. The stories of selfless acts and love fill me with hope for our future. It starts with you and me - being love, being joy, being enlightened. We can be the change we want to see and then together we can raise the consciousness of the communities we are part of and eventually the country we live in and beyond. If we turned off the negative media, they would soon learn that it is

---

4 David Hawkins book 'The Map of Consciousness Explained' shares the levels of consciousness and the scale of emotions that can move us to enlightenment.

unacceptable to continue to deliver biased, unsubstantiated, scandalous stories. We deserve fully-balanced solution-focused information.

The way our society is transforming in the 21st century is following the research of Dr Clare Graves, which is being continued by Don Beck of *Spiral Dynamics*[5] as we enter into the *teal layer* of his Evolutionary Level of Needs. In other words we are emerging into a level of self-organising. Here, potentially, societies will no longer require governing, can potentially self-govern, providing the culture and agreed rules of engagement are met. In essence, what we are instigating in the *Collaboration Global* community.

I doubt I will see this in my lifetime but if *Collaboration Global* could replicate a facsimile of what it might look like, imagine what the world could become.

Or perhaps more relevantly to you, if you knew how to replicate a self-organising team in your business, along the lines described in this book, imagine how fulfilled and empowered your staff would be. They in turn would share the joy of working in your organisation and you would never have a recruitment issue again, they would also become your advocates as they raved about working in your organisation and they would willingly volunteer to do the work they love. You would then do more of what you love, which is why you started the business in the first place.

Practice it at home too, there are no boundaries to a collaborative mindset.

Ultimately, if you always do what you've always done, you will always get what you always got.

---

5 Spiral Dynamics https://en.wikipedia.org/wiki/Spiral_Dynamics

Either Henry Ford, Albert Einstein, or someone said it first, but it still fits here. We cannot afford the luxury of doing what we always did, that is a sure-fire way to insanity. We cannot return to 'normal' after the pandemic, that no longer exists, we have to create a new normal and by empowering each other through collaboration we can raise the collective consciousness and discover a whole new way of being. Better for the individual, for relationships, for businesses, for organisations and for communities.

Time for transformation from the ground floor UP!

Chapter 14

HOW CAN WE MAKE A DIFFERENCE?

Huge responsibility, right? Too big to handle?

Let's take it down to bite-sized pieces, what can you be responsible for?

Start with YOU!

Connect to who you are, not the façade you put out to the world, the real you, the you that maybe you haven't fully discovered yet.

Start by asking yourself these questions:

- What do I love to do?
- What am I amazing at? - your genius, don't be modest
- Do I enjoy/love what I am good at? - not always the same thing
- What is my purpose?
- What is my mission?
- What do I believe?

- What are my values?
- What is important to me?
- What is there in my life I need to transform?
- Who in my life is in my support team?
- What is missing from my life?
- What are my limiting beliefs?
- What triggers me?
- What is my joy?
- Why am I here?

Now be honest, were you surprised by any of the answers? It often helps to go through some of these basic questions with a professional, they have years of experience of honing in on what might be blocking the answers from flowing. If you have never experienced a coaching session, you will be blown away by the profound experience it can be.

It will highlight for you whether you are currently living up to your full potential. Then, what you want to consider is whether you are 'collaboration ready'. That is part of the beauty of *Collaboration Global*, you get to practice collaboration in a safe loving environment, handy if you have yet to undertake any personal development.

Collaborations have the habit of showing the cracks early on. I love seeing what triggers people, knowing my own peculiar quirks, and if you don't understand your own I can guarantee you will have had ridiculous unnecessary arguments because of the lack of understanding over why you get triggered.

Once you have done some of the groundwork, you can connect to your higher being - BE the change you want to see. It doesn't come automatically, we have to work at it. Be the example of what you want to see in others. So, if you want a great husband, choose to be a great wife and vice versa. Deliver what you want to receive and see what happens. Without having an argument, your partner will (subconsciously) slowly see a difference in you and adapt accordingly, and you find you get a partner upgrade.

Yes, I know that is an extremely simplified explanation, I would need a whole other book to demonstrate transformation of your BEING, but then that is what the *Collaboration Global* community is for, to help each other learn and apply our learning. Meanwhile Brené Brown is probably a good author to start your journey.

Once you have chosen this path, you will want to have people around to support you. We are the average of the five people we most associate with. We often look at that statement with reference to money, but it goes much deeper than that. Look around you, who are your friends, colleagues, family? Are they generally negative or positive? Spend some time listening to what they say. Do they listen to you or are they simply waiting to respond and trump your story? What do they read, what TV do they watch, who are their heroes?

Now I am not saying get rid of your friends, but please be aware of how they might be influencing you negatively, without you even realising it. Accept them for who they are, but don't let their lifestyle be your lifestyle, if they are not inspiring you.

If we are going to have a better life, make a positive impact for others and be responsible for creating a better planet, then we can only do this by starting with ourselves.

Chapter 15

IF NOT US, THEN WHO?

I don't know about you, but I struggle with all of the pain in the world and used to feel impotent to do anything about it.

It wasn't until the *Collaboration Global* community started to grow and the possibilities that afforded to me, did I begin to consider that actually I and many others can actually make a global difference. I am continually looking for people to partner and collaborate with, who are of the same mind and I am continually blown away by the good that I find in the world - my world.

I know I am taking baby steps to make a difference, but collectively we can crack the code. I have seen collaboration and the collaborative mindset transform the lives of individuals again and again. I have seen those individuals take their learning and utilise it in their business and, indeed, take it out to other associations and organisations to help them too. It works, taking the collaborative mindset and walking away from the WIIFM (*What's In It For Me?*) mindset, leaving it in the 20th century.

If nothing else, when we consider our individual choices as we purchase our food and clothing and consider our collective choices as we move around our planet, mindful of coronavirus, if we consider who we are being, what message we want to leave, what our personal and collective legacy will be - then we will make a difference! Together!

We must be mindful of our future generations as they face the fall out of our selfish consumption, which has been damaging our planet since the Industrial Revolution.

Now is the time to join the dots, from the causes of poor mental health, to our overstretched health service, to the money moguls who get away with murder, to Greta Thunberg and the devastation of our planet. All are connected as we work out how to tackle them.

YOU can make a difference! TOGETHER! We Are Stronger!

This way of thinking will bring the quadruple win!

Win - for you, watch your relationships blossom.

Win for your business - create a powerhouse of positivity.

Win for your clients - teach them your secret and pay it forward.

Win for our planet - raise the consciousness of everyone we connect to.

One solution,

COLLABORATE!

Conclusion: What next?

Become *A Collaborator In Action!*

If any of this message has resonated with you, we would love you to get in touch and become part of our growing *Collaboration Global* community:

A place where you can learn about yourself, understand better the nuances of collaboration and see how you can support and be supported as you make an impact on our world.

By having *Collaboration Global* as part of your network you can help more people, and by making collaboration part of your business and your life, you will see your world transform every day.

We can choose to carry on living our life as though we are apart from each other and separate from the problems of our world or acknowledge that we are deeply connected with humanity and are responsible for our part in it and be part of the change we seek.

What will you choose?

Join us as our guest at a live Zoom meeting every month and meet our community.

Book through Eventbrite

https://www.eventbrite.co.uk/e/collaboration-global-online-meeting-tickets-126034802487?aff=ebdssbonlinesearch

Or visit our website for more information

https://collaborationglobal.org/

REFERENCES

- Be More Pirate - Sam Conniff Allende
- 7 Habits of Highly Successful People - Stephen Covey
- Chimp Paradox - Professor Steve Peters
- Spiral Dynamics - Clare Graves and Don Beck
- The Emotion Code - David Hawkins

Books/People That Have Influenced Me

- Spiral Dynamics - Don Beck
- Pendulum - Roy Williams and Michael Drew
- Non Zero Sum, The Logic of Human Destiny - Robert Wright
- We Think - Charles Leadbeater
- The Shift, The Future of Work is Already Here - Lynda Gratton
- The Art of Possibility - Benjamin Zander
- The Click - Ori and Rom Brafman

WITH SPECIAL THANKS TO

My husband Alan who has been my rock for every day that we have been together. I couldn't have a better person on my side.

My daughters Dani and Nicci who inspire me to be better every day.

The *Collaboration Global* community, without your faith in me and this Movement we would not have created the amazing space we all know and love.

Together we can achieve EVERYTHING!

ABOUT GILL TINEY

Gill has spent her life struggling to understand why the world is such an unfair place. From seeing how homeless people were treated in the Housing Dept of the Greater London Council when she was just 16, to witnessing the disparity between able bodied children to those who needed specialist learning support and yet didn't qualify, when she was a teacher at 36.

In between she learned the fundamentals of running her business and was appalled at the attitude of some business owners who were prepared to gain success at any costs to those they met on their journey. Life wasn't fair and she couldn't reconcile herself to that. Starting her third business in 2007, she vowed to do it differently.

Finally, after years of personal development, business growth and experimenting with the concept of collaboration she founded *Collaboration Global* in 2019. Not only is this community a place for individuals to understand themselves better and to stretch their thinking, it is also a place where like minded and like hearted people can come together to support each other to success.

She is building the world she wants to see, walking the talk and asking others to join her on that journey.

This is her fourth book, she also hosts the *Being Human* podcast, publishes an online magazine, *The Quest* and is a speaker and business coach. Her passion is the community at *Collaboration Global* where she sees the future of business evolving and a culture of love, connection and abundance being the bedrock of our new world.

Contact Gill Tiney

gill@collaborationglobal.org

collaborationglobal.org

Printed in Dunstable, United Kingdom

80800579R00092